BlacKkKlansman

TIMECODES

A book series exploring individual movies minute by minute.

Series Editors

Nicholas Rombes, University of Detroit Mercy, USA
Nadine Boljkovac, University of Colorado, USA

Advisory Board

Paweł Frelik (University of Warsaw, Poland)
Andrew Gallix (Independent Scholar, France)
Colleen Kennedy-Karpat (Bilkent University, Turkey)
Shiva Moghanloo (Independent Scholar, Iran)
Björn Sonnenberg-Schrank (Heinrich Heine University
Düsseldorf, Germany)
Steven Shaviro (Wayne State University, USA)
Constantine Verevis (Monash University, Australia)

Alex Zamalin is Professor of Africana Studies and Political Science at Rutgers University-New Brunswick. He is the author of several books, including *Antiracism: An Introduction* (2019), *Black Utopia: The History of an Idea from Black Nationalism to Afrofuturism* (2019) and *Against Civility: The Hidden Racism in Our Obsession with Civility* (2021).

Also in the Series:

Gerry: Movies Minute by Minute, by
Nicholas Rombes

BlacKkKlansman

Movies Minute by Minute

Alex Zamalin

BLOOMSBURY ACADEMIC
NEW YORK · LONDON · OXFORD · NEW DELHI · SYDNEY

BLOOMSBURY ACADEMIC
Bloomsbury Publishing Inc
1385 Broadway, New York, NY 10018, USA
50 Bedford Square, London, WC1B 3DP, UK
29 Earlsfort Terrace, Dublin 2, Ireland

BLOOMSBURY, BLOOMSBURY ACADEMIC and the Diana logo are
trademarks of Bloomsbury Publishing Plc

First published in the United States of America 2025

Copyright © Alex Zamalin, 2025

Cover design: Eleanor Rose
Cover illustration © Freya Betts

Bloomsbury Publishing Inc does not have any control over, or responsibility
for, any third-party websites referred to or in this book. All internet
addresses given in this book were correct at the time of going to
press. The author and publisher regret any inconvenience caused if
addresses have changed or sites have ceased to exist, but can accept
no responsibility for any such changes.

Library of Congress Cataloging-in-Publication Data
Names: Zamalin, Alex, 1986- author.
Title: BlacKkKansman: movies minute by minute / Alex Zamalin.
Description: New York: Bloomsbury Academic, 2025. | Series: Timecodes;
vol. 1 | Includes index.
Identifiers: LCCN 2024028394 (print) | LCCN 2024028395 (ebook) |
ISBN 9798765103807 (paperback) | ISBN 9798765103814 (hardback) |
ISBN 9798765103845 (ebook) | ISBN 9798765103838 (pdf)
Subjects: LCSH: BlacKkKlansman (Motion picture)
Classification: LCC PN1997.2.B575 Z36 2025 (print) | LCC PN1997.2.B575
(ebook) | DDC 791.43/72–dc23/eng/20240724
LC record available at https://lccn.loc.gov/2024028394
LC ebook record available at https://lccn.loc.gov/2024028395

ISBN: HB: 979-8-7651-0381-4
PB: 979-8-7651-0380-7
ePDF: 979-8-7651-0383-8
eBook: 979-8-7651-0384-5

Series: Timecodes

Typeset by Deanta Global Publishing Services, Chennai, India
Printed and bound in Great Britain

To find out more about our authors and books visit www.bloomsbury.com
and sign up for our newsletters.

CONTENTS

Preface vi

Minutes 1–128 1

Notes 97
Index 100

PREFACE

Few films speak to their historical moment as powerfully as Spike Lee's *BlacKkKlansman*. Even fewer, however, are made with the aim of directly addressing a third rail in American politics: race. In telling the autobiographical story of how one Black police officer covertly infiltrated the Ku Klux Klan in Colorado Springs, Colorado, in the early 1970s, *BlacKkKlansman* accomplishes both objectives. The film is a remarkable study of how racism operates in the United States amid the growing public concern about white nationalism in the aftermath of Donald Trump's election as president in 2016. In offering an answer to this question, *BlacKkKlansman* is also a roadmap for an alternative world where antiracism flourishes.

I first saw *BlacKkKlansman* online in 2018. I didn't see it in theaters because, knowing something about Spike Lee's cinematic style—the turns of phrase, the color schemes, the music—I wanted to experience it on my own, and in my own time. To pause it. To rewind it. To scrutinize each frame. Appreciate each visual composition. When I first watched Lee's classic *Do the Right Thing* (1989), for instance, in college as an aspiring intellectual, I was not yet prepared for Lee's style and his unflinching approach to everything. But the film washed over me nonetheless. The unforgettable rhythm of Public Enemy's song "Fight the Power," which begins the movie and pulsates throughout; the streets of Brooklyn, which I knew well from my childhood where I grew up; the hard-nosed New York style, through and through, which I understood personally. But *BlacKkKlansman* hit different in 2018. By then, I wasn't a college student. I was a professor at a university in Detroit and an expert in American racial politics. A Spike Lee movie—and I had watched many by that time—was no longer a cinematic feast to simply enjoy but an object of careful consideration to study, which I knew, in some way, would intersect with themes in my own research.

There were rumblings that Lee was about to release a new film to address the Trump era, but I still had lots of questions. How would Lee frame white supremacy at a moment when it was being widely discussed? Would Lee maintain his no-holds-barred approach to racism? In 1989, for example, when Lee directed *Do the Right Thing*, his targets were clear, but so was his status as a social critic. American politics had veered right. It was the long decade of Ronald Reagan. Talk of being tough on crime-dominated political campaigns, prisons were being built at an exponential rate, social services were being cut left and right, and "color-blindness" was beginning to dominate how Americans talked about race. In addressing anti-Black police violence, Black rebellion, the prospects of Black solidarity, and the ongoing reality of white racism, *Do the Right Thing* took up themes that were, undoubtedly, being marginalized in the mainstream.

2018, the year *BlacKkKlansman* was released, was remarkably different. Hate crimes had skyrocketed for the previous two years. Donald Trump's racist rhetoric around immigrants and people of color made front-page news. And, perhaps, most significantly, Americans were exposed to the horrors of the "Unite the Right" white supremacist rally in Charlottesville, Virginia, on August 12, 2017. The rally left a white antiracist protester, Heather Heyer, dead, many injured, and a city torn to shreds. The Charlottesville march saw hundreds of white supremacists descending upon the city, with tiki torches in hand (some even openly carried swastikas), chanting "Jews will not replace us!" and "Blood and Soil," terms that recalled the language of neo-Nazis and fascists. Forced to speak on the implications of the rally, the then president Trump, on the very same day, infamously excused some of its white nationalism—most of the protesters, he declared, were peaceful and upstanding citizens. Trump then went on to create an equivalence between the racists and antiracists—there were bad people on both sides, he claimed. Many Americans who watched the events unfold in Charlottesville were stunned. Aghast. How could this violence and hate happen here? Is this what the United States had now become? Is this the path down which the United States was rapidly descending?

As I watched Charlottesville unfold, I did not know the answer to these questions. Yes, as a scholar, I had long been familiar with the histories of right-wing racist violence (enslavement, the chain gang, lynching, bombings, voter intimidation, cross burnings) and the ways right-wing politicians (from proslavery US senator John C. Calhoun in the 1830s to Republican Richard Nixon in the 1960s) would exonerate or condone such violence. I knew that the far-right had always been a force in American politics and American history. But I did not expect to see hundreds of racists, emboldened, descend upon a college town, Charlottesville, in broad daylight, with a sense of optimism and hope that a new era—under the presidency of Trump—was upon us. With *BlacKkKlansman*, it's clear that Lee didn't want Trump or the far-right to have the last word on that day, or what was to come in its wake. *BlacKkKlansman* was released on August 10, 2018—roughly, the one-year anniversary of the Charlottesville rally.

Watching *BlacKkKlansman* is a unique experience. When I first saw the movie, knowing it was loosely based on a true story, hearing about the positive critical response and the 6-minute standing ovation it received at the Cannes Film Festival during its premiere, I was struck by the mash-up of genres. It's a comedy, drama, melodrama, thriller, police procedural, buddy film, and romance, with elements of magical realism, *noir,* and western. And yet, although *BlacKkKlansman* freely borrows from different styles, the tone of the film is singular and clear: it is unapologetically political and argumentative. It speaks directly to the viewer in ways that are far from subtle.

PREFACE ix

Each word, sentence, and image is carefully crafted to make an observation from an antiracist perspective. In this way, *BlacKkKlansman* felt like a Spike Lee movie. But in other ways, it was different. Lee was no longer the Socratic gadfly trying to destroy American orthodoxies of democratic exceptionalism or pierce holes through the veneer of American equality. Racism and white supremacy were no longer something that was on the periphery of American discourse. After Trump and Charlottesville, they were the discourse. And no one could look away.

In its effort to both entertain and inform the public about how we got here, *BlacKkKlansman* tackles US history and is a work of antiracist filmmaking. It at once informs Americans about their racist cultural history and explains how their social and political history has led them to their present moment. On the one hand, *BlacKkKlansman* reminds viewers that American filmmaking has a long and racist history—the movie begins with clips from *Gone with the Wind* (1939), which imagines the white South during the Civil War (1861–5) and Reconstruction era (1865–77) as a heroic place, to the end of the film, which shows clips of *Birth of a Nation* (1915), D. W. Griffith's racist depiction of post-Reconstruction America, and the rise of the Ku Klux Klan. On the other hand, *BlacKkKlansman* also turns to a particular moment in history in the aftermath of the Civil Rights Movement—in the early 1970s—to remind the viewer how much of what we see today is a product and legacy of that moment. For example, when white resentment began to percolate, when coded racist language became mainstreamed, when the right had to drop its hoods and put on suits, when Black Power was crushed by the state, and white nationalism began to quietly flourish underground. In telling this story, *BlacKkKlansman* inevitably produces a counter-story of both American culture and a counter-narrative of American politics. By telling this story from his unique perspective as a Black filmmaker, Lee refuses to allow racist images and narratives to saturate American film. By drawing a direct line from the 1970s to 2018, Lee undermines the idea of America as a nation that always progressively moves toward equality, freedom, and justice. By presenting how antiracism might be made real—through images of successful Black politics and Black freedom throughout the film—Lee complicates the direction US history might yet move.

Just like Spike Lee's films, and all books for that matter, this book brings a particular perspective to its subject matter. There are many ways to examine *BlacKkKlansman*—its inventive visual style, didactic argumentative structure, use of music, and cinematic movement. But in this book, I read the work through the lens of political theory. The dialogue, visuals, sound, and movement became a way for me to examine questions that are of significant concern to citizens and political actors. For instance, what is the meaning of freedom under social constraint? How do racism and anti-Blackness structure the parameters of conversation and belonging? Is redistribution or recognition crucial for justice? Is power dispersed, and, if it is, how must resistance be decentralized? What is political about speech, and how exactly does language have a performative political function? How to build solidarity and imagine political commitment? What is antiracism? How can it be achieved politically?

Because it has compelling, sophisticated answers to these questions at a moment when these questions are of pressing concern, *BlacKkKlansman* deserves our attention. Now and in the future.

Minutes 1–128

Minute 1

BlacKkKlansman begins with a clip of the white Southern aristocrat, Scarlett O'Hara, walking through a field of dead Confederate soldiers during the Civil War—this is the 1939 film adaption of Margaret Mitchell's "Lost Cause" novel, *Gone with the Wind* (1936), which imagines the Civil War as a conflict over state's rights and Southern traditions, rather than slavery—uttering to herself, lost in thought and gripped by grief, "God save the confederacy." To begin this way is to suggest that racism is not simply maintained through bad political institutions or structural economic inequalities. But it is sustained by narratives—fantasies and myths that form the core of identity, like the one O'Hara and many white people tell themselves. Once slavery, or segregation, or lynching, or mass incarceration, or police brutality is retold by white people as a melodramatic story of flawed but good people simply trying to keep their communities safe, to protect their loved ones, or of heroic men and women fighting for causes they believe to be just, you can obscure how racism dominates, represses, and murders those who are racialized. When the camera zooms out, and we see Alec Baldwin, as the character Dr. Kennebrew Beauregard, the white supremacist, turning to the white viewer and reminding them they have "lost the battle but not the war," Lee is suggesting the violent power of narrative construction is still with us. From the perspective of racism, an individual "battle" may be won or lost, which is to say, legislation might be passed to mitigate discrimination or norms might change about race. But the long war is waged through how white people imagine race, themselves, and their country. *BlacKkKlansman* is a work of political filmmaking because of its unapologetic attempt to realize essayist James Baldwin's view that "America" must "be forced to re-examine themselves and release themselves from many things that are now taken to be sacred, and to discard nearly all the assumptions that have been used to justify their lives and their anguish and their crimes so long."

Minute 2

In minute 2, Beauregard looks squarely at the viewer. Projected over his face and in the background is a video of the Little Rock Nine, the first Black students to racially integrate Little Rock Central High School in Arkansas in 1957. This is in the wake of the Supreme Court's *Brown v. Board of Education* (1954) decision to render Jim Crow segregation in public schooling unconstitutional. "Miscegenation and integration," Beauregard says, is the "final nail in a black coffin towards America becoming a mongrel nation." Minute 2 lays bare the tyrannical and totalizing force of racism upon the inner lives of racists. Racism cannot admit any interracial love, cannot allow children to go to school with one another—but also poses a question to the viewer. Beauregard isn't just articulating a view, uttering a few words that can be dismissed. He is livid, inflamed by emotion. His very sense of self comes alive, feels real, precisely in imbibing racism. If white phobia of the Black other, and the emotions it stirs—hate, resentment—gives rise to a coherent sense of self—then racism cannot be overcome— as some liberals optimistically believe—through more facts about our common humanity, greater sensitivity training, more compassion, or greater tolerance. The racist wants to feel angry, needs to terrify everyone around him. Irrationality and madness are not side effects; they are the point.

"There are people who are attracted by the durability of a stone," writes Jean-Paul Sartre in his *Anti-Semite and Jew*: "They wish to be massive and impenetrable; they wish to be massive they wish not to change. Where, indeed, would change take them? . . . Since the [racist] has chosen hate, we are forced to conclude that it is the state of passion that he loves."[1]

Minute 3

White supremacy's secret arsenal involves playing the victim card. The racist professes nostalgia for an imagined past that never was but to which he feels firmly attached. Once the image crumbles—as it inevitably will—the racist takes on the position of the aggrieved, the wronged. This fuels their rage. It amplifies their conviction in righteous violence. Beauregard repeats, "We had a great way of life," over and over again, breathlessly, "until MLK and his army of commies" destroyed it. He then shows racist images from D. W. Griffith's 1915 film,

The Birth of a Nation, which depicts white actors in blackface as zealous and bloodthirsty in their lust for subduing and assaulting. Beauregard asserts that Black citizens are "rapists, murders, craving the virgin pure flesh of white women," calling them "super predators." They are being led by "high-ranking, blood-sucking Jews." Beauregard's words are shocking and disturbing, but they aren't new. To unleash their reign of terror, racists preemptively depict those they dominate as the aggressors. Long before contemporary right-wing talk of the "great replacement"—the idea, for instance, that Democratic elites collude with nonwhite migrant populations to change the racial demographics of the country and dilute the power of the white electorate—the racist has always painted the Black, brown, Jewish, and nonwhite citizen as the nefarious one who preys on the innocence and goodwill of the racist. The racist knows what they are doing. He consciously reverses the roles. The oppressor is the victim; the victim is the oppressor.

Minute 4

The camera cuts to an aerial shot of the Rocky Mountains in Colorado, a geographic area in the Mountain West, ostensibly free from Jim Crow segregation. This is, at a moment, in the 1970s, when—according to some—the "race problem" has been solved with the passage of the Civil Rights Act of 1964, the Voting Rights Act of 1965, and the Fair Housing Act of 1968. A young Black man, Ron Stallworth (played by John David Washington), notices a sign that says "Join the Colorado Springs Police Force: Minorities encouraged to apply." He looks up, fixes his black hair, and smiles with a sense of self-assurance. The advertisement for law enforcement, as well as Stallworth's attempt to groom himself before a job interview, is a perfect illustration of the liberal logic of racial justice. To end racial inequality, liberalism suggests, Black citizens must be incorporated and assimilated into the mainstream: they must be good soldiers, patriots, cops, or middle-class earners. This version of liberalism, however, comes with a twist: it at once displaces responsibility for the white majority to address the histories of anti-Black dehumanization and places it exclusively upon the shoulders of exemplary Black citizens to prove their worth in the marketplace. The result? Gone are more radical antiracist projects like defunding the police, confronting racial capitalism, or abolishing global imperialism. Instead, Black citizens' assimilation into the nation is used to elevate the unjust status quo and deflect focus away from abolishing structures of domination. Incorporation, minute 4 illustrates, is the way to silence radical critique.

Minute 5

Minute 5 reveals what the movie will outline, but what many white Americans are often unwilling to accept. Racial assimilation is often destined to fail—it is no match for a racist culture. In a stunning reversal of expectations, Stallworth's interview looks more like a criminal interrogation. The presumption of guilt is front and center, and the exemplary citizen, the "model minority," must continually prove their status. The interrogators—in other words, the establishment—get to define what counts as normal or what is acceptable. A Black cop and a white cop take turns asking: "why weren't you drafted into the Vietnam War?" "Do you do drugs, are you a womanizer?" That Stallworth answers every question impeccably is beside the point. The real question, the one his employment hinges upon, is not his qualifications or character, but his willingness to tolerate radical forms of dehumanization. The Black cop cuts to the chase—"How would you feel if another cop called you a n---?" Stallworth must acquiesce, must shrug it off as no big deal. He has no choice. This is because—in the aftermath of the 1960s, and the end of de jure racism—the presumption is of racial progress.

It is normalized and unquestioned. Stallworth must give the white racist cop the benefit of the doubt—"he didn't mean it, he was just joking"—because the price of Black assimilation is Black respectability and compassion.

Minute 6

The interview/interrogation continues in minute 6, which now begins to take on a comical tone. The unnamed Black police officer interviewing him tells Stallworth that he thinks he would be an ideal figure to create a more inclusive police department. Stallworth would be, as he puts it, "Jackie Robinson," and the white police chief, Bridges, will be "your Branch Rickey" (the Major League Baseball team, Brooklyn Dodgers' manager who managed Robinson). Bridges interrupts to remind Stallworth of this inconvenient truth: the weight of this assignment will be on "you, and you alone." To draw a parallel between a Black man joining the Colorado Springs Police Department and Jackie Robinson as the first Black man to integrate Major League Baseball is, on the face of it, a farce. Robinson was a national symbol, while Stallworth is simply looking for gainful employment. Stallworth is uninterested in being a spokesperson for his race, and even if he were interested in such a pursuit, the parallel between Major League Baseball and the Colorado Springs Police Department makes little sense. And yet, the fact that these kinds of metaphors of racial integration are so freely tossed around speaks to the impossibility of integration, and the poverty of conceptualizing Black freedom. Stallworth is not asked whether he actually wants to be Jackie Robinson, whether he has any interest in that role. He is instead forced to assume the role with all its responsibility. He is not asked, he is told, that his identity will be structured in the following way, that his status—in the white imagination—is preemptively defined for him. In the white imagination, the Robinson metaphor is never critically scrutinized—as if there is no difference between being a Black baseball player and a Black police officer when it comes to Black equality. And, perhaps, as minute 6 aims to tell us, this is precisely the point: if one believes Black citizens do not have a say in whether they want to be Jackie Robinson at all times—they are always judged as if they are; or there is no difference between equality in sports and in law enforcement, or, for that matter, in any realm of life—then the question of Black freedom and subjectivity becomes erased. Within this context, Stallworth's desires—maybe he's apolitical? Maybe he doesn't want the burden? Maybe he just wants to work? Maybe he doesn't want to represent, or be the spokesperson for his race?—are incomprehensible to white citizens.

Minute 7

Throughout much of his writings, the Black essayist James Baldwin would offer an astute interpretation of racism. The racist Black image in the white mind tells us less about the fact of Black character and more about the anxieties, fears, and uncertainties of the very white people who displace these feelings and attributes from themselves and project them upon Black people they've never met or known. Baldwin writes in his essay "Many Thousands Gone" that

> the ways in which the Negro has affected the American psychology are betrayed in our popular culture and in our morality; in our estrangement from him is the depth of our estrangement from ourselves. We cannot ask: what do we *really* feel about him—such a question merely opens the gates on chaos. What we really feel about him is involved with all that we feel about everything, about everyone, about ourselves.[2]

Racism, in this way, tells us more about what the racist believes than the identity of those they racialize. After all, those who

8   BLACKKKLANSMAN

are racialized do not invest countless hours contorting their identities to conform to these grotesque images (of criminality, violence, hypersexuality, crookedness, anger). And even if some people did act in these ways some of the time, one cannot possibly capture the complexity of any human life in these myopic terms. A visual representation of this point is on display in minute 7. Stallworth approaches a white police officer avoiding clerical work. The officer is looking at a *Life* magazine profile of Hollywood actress Cybill Shepherd. "What do you think?" asks the cop. "I think she's a good actress," Stallworth replies. "Oh, come on," the cop replies in a playful tone, attempting to bond with Stallworth, "You know you want some of that." Of the two, the only person objectifying and sexualizing Shepherd is the white cop. But in the cop's mind, it's clearly Stallworth. On the one hand, this continues a long trope, dating back to the post-Reconstruction era, in which Black men were imagined as hypersexual and especially attracted to white women (the myth was popularized in Thomas Dixon's novel, *The Leopard's Spots* [1902], which became the basis for Griffith's *The Birth of a Nation*). On the other hand, the cop's racist projection onto Stallworth is, in his mind, precisely what creates a masculine bond between the two men. The white cop's conviction that Stallworth is, undoubtedly, attracted to white women reinforces a patriarchal worldview that denigrates women. Stallworth, for his part, is thus stuck in an impossible place. If he agrees with the cop, then his hypersexuality is confirmed, and patriarchy is culturally reinforced. If he doesn't, then he is seen as too confrontational, angry, oppositional (all racist images that mark Black identity). Stuck in an impossible situation, Stallworth says nothing in response.

Minute 8

Stallworth walks into Chief Bridges's office and says he would like to do serious police work, perhaps becoming an undercover detective. Confused, the chief asks, "what, narcotics?" "You think a lot of yourself, don't you?" Notice here how racism circumscribes Stallworth's subjectivity. He is presumed to be interested in pursuing a specific kind of criminal activity, narcotics (as if a Black officer would somehow have insider knowledge in drug trafficking, even though drug addiction is as widespread in white communities as it is in Black communities). At the same time, this presumption is attached to the idea that Stallworth is too excessive in his desires—that he is uninterested in being like everyone else, that he wants more than his fair share, that his ego is inflated. In the racist imagination, Black citizens are everything at once—hyper-deficient in their morals (Stallworth has insider knowledge about narcotics) and hyper-excessive in their desires to be exceptional (Stallworth has inflated self-worth). This contradiction explains why racism has no inherent rational structure. Racism cannot be reasoned with. There is no consistency in the racist image—the racialized subject is and is not the same thing at once. To quote James Baldwin again, who, reflecting on the racist images of Aunt Jemima and Uncle Tom as metaphors for race in the United States, so eloquently describes the madness of racism:

> There was no one more forbearing than Aunt Jemima, no one stronger or more pious or more loyal or more wise; there was, at the same time, no one weaker or more faithless or more vicious and certainly no one more immoral. Uncle Tom, trustworthy and sexless, needed only to drop the title "Uncle" to become violent, crafty, and sullen, a menace to any white woman who passed by ... Aunt Jemima and Uncle Tom, our creations, at the last evaded us; they had a life— their own, perhaps a better life than ours—and they would never tell us what it was ... what depths of contempt, what heights of indifference, what prodigies of resilience, what untamable superiority allowed them so vividly to endure, neither perishing nor rising up in a body to wipe us from the earth, the image perpetually shattered and the word failed.[3]

Minute 9

During minute 9, Stallworth begins to act on a recognition that finally becomes clear to him: one cannot easily reason with a racist. After multiple white officers in the CSPD refer to Black men as "toads," as they ask Stallworth to find records in the office, Stallworth—for the first time in the film—powerfully resists his dehumanization. "There are no toads here, only human beings," he says. Racism relies on bad faith, which is to say that the racist asserts something they know is patently false. Deep down, the racist knows Black citizens are human, but they nonetheless take great pleasure in describing them in subhuman ways, precisely because it forces the Black citizen to "prove" their humanity—which is, of course, humiliating. This vicious cycle frames the possibilities for antiracist action. For this reason, the nineteenth-century Black abolitionist Frederick Douglass, at the height of US slavery in 1852, argued in "What to the Slave Is the Fourth of July?" (1852) that in order to confront the racist, rational argument is insufficient, or even useless. What is necessary in the response is irony, fire, and brimstone. "At a time like this," Douglass says in his lecture,

> scorching irony, not convincing argument, is needed. O! had I the ability, and could reach the nation's ear, I would, to-day, pour out a fiery stream of biting ridicule, blasting reproach, withering sarcasm, and stern rebuke. For it is not light that is needed, but fire; it is not the gentle shower, but thunder. We need the storm, the whirlwind, and the earthquake.[4]

This theoretical insight cannot be overstated. To confront racism, one needs to put the racist on the defensive—lay bare their bad faith. That's why Stallworth looks the cop straight in the eye and simply declares what is obvious to everyone—"there are no toads here." Notice how Stallworth does not defend his—or Black people's—humanity. Instead, he draws attention to what the white cop knows but refuses to admit, as his colleague, a Black officer, stands directly before him—that Black people are not toads.

Minute 10

Stallworth takes his time in fulfilling the task demanded of him. He walks slowly, puts the record in his mouth, and drops it on the desk, listlessly. "Was that respectful enough for you, officer Toad?", the cop, Andy Landers, remarks, walking away, smiling, as he shuts the door. As he leaves, Stallworth does air karate, pretending to fight him. What to make of this dynamic? Did Stallworth avoid conflict? Miss an opportunity for resistance? To the contrary. How we answer these questions depends on what we see, and what we do not see. In his classic work, *Domination and the Arts of Resistance* (1990), the political scientist James Scott suggests that dominated people resist behind closed doors, in ways often not legible to those in power. These "hidden transcripts," as Scott puts it, are actions that take place "offstage, beyond direct observation by powerholders."[5] From this vantage point, acts of resistance are not always dramatic but exist in the everyday—they include poking fun at the oppressors, criticizing power, and building solidarity and networks of resistance behind closed doors. In this way, then, Stallworth is working from within the hidden transcript—with no one around, he is sharpening his tools of critique. But such work is not trivial. It is meaningful precisely because it preserves the oppressor's dignity and, as a form of self-work, discloses to the colonized their capacity for freedom and direct action. According to historian Robin D. G. Kelley, everyday political acts in the Jim Crow South—something as minor as chewing gum on a segregated bus or talking loudly in a crowded room—were subversive activities that, over time, toppled racial authoritarianism. The more dominated citizens picked apart the system, the more emboldened they became to organize and carry out a mass movement—like the Civil

Rights movement—which had an explicitly political objective. Not all resistance is the same, but everyday resistance cannot be discounted because it is both a form of micropolitical action and a training ground for larger goals. As Kelley writes in his book, *Race Rebels: Culture, Politics, and the Black Working Class* (1994), history that

> "emphasizes the infrapolitics of the black working class requires that we substantially redefine politics. Too often politics is defined by how people participate rather than why; by traditional definition the question of what is political hinges on whether or not groups are involved in elections, political parties, or grass-roots social movements. Yet the how seems far less important than the why, since many of the so-called real political institutions have not always proved effective for, or even accessible to, oppressed people.[6]

Minute 11

The camera cuts to somewhere in the wilderness. We see a barren landscape, marked by tranquillity. The next shot is of a phone ringing inside a house, disrupting this peace. Stallworth wakes up early in the morning and picks up this phone. He's disoriented, rudely awakened, since he isn't expecting to be on the clock. Bridges is on the other line, says he has reconsidered. He would like to give him a special assignment, after all. Knowing that he can't refuse, Stallworth immediately gets dressed and runs out the door. In minute 11, the ringing phone, as an interruption, gives us a sense of the politics of time. Stallworth must always be ready for the assignment and never be late, whereas Bridges is the sovereign who can interpret time, has freedom in how he manipulates time. What is the meaning and function of time under a condition of domination? According to Karl Marx, capitalism has a tyrannical reach over the worker's experience of time and subjectivity—subject to the demands of profit-making, the worker is being enlisted to work in order to meet the demands of the production schedule, which shifts with the whims of the employer.[7] This condition of alienation is especially acute under conditions of racialized capitalism. Black workers are exploited as both workers and racialized citizens. As a worker, Stallworth must be ready to interrupt his schedule to maintain his employment; as a Black worker, subject to racist assumptions of his incompetence, Stallworth must work harder than everyone. His sense of time cannot be his own if he is to survive. Even still, survival is not the same as freedom. "CP time?" Bridges asks, when Stallworth arrives in his office. "The rookie is late."

Minute 12

"As far as I'm concerned," Bridges tells Stallworth when he arrives to work, "FBI Director J Edgar Hoover was dead right to say the Black Panthers are the greatest internal threat to the security of these United States." His undercover assignment, Bridges tells Stallworth, is to infiltrate a speech by Black Panther Stokely Carmichael (Kwame Ture), who is speaking at a local college campus later that night. "We don't want this Carmichael getting into the minds of good black people here in Colorado Springs and stirring them up," Bridges declares emphatically. Minute 12 reminds viewers of the long-standing US government's obsession with crushing Black radicalism. Black Lives Matter is demonized by the political right today (recall, for instance, that under Donald Trump's administration, the FBI defined aspects of the movement as a national security threat, under the totalizing and obscure language of "Black Identity Extremism"). Half a century earlier, the Black Panthers, founded in 1966, in an effort to promote Black self-defense and self-determination, were at the forefront of Republican president Richard Nixon's talk of "law and order," of cracking down on crime. The function of this is clear. Defining Black radicalism, centered on economic equality and protection of the Black community from police brutality, as a form of domestic extremism, is an attempt to criminalize Black politics and thus make any talk of Black liberation forbidden. By focusing on these imagined threats, the right ensures that the state diverts attention from the true existential threats and domestic terrorists—white supremacists who want to annihilate nonwhite citizens and hold no respect for the sovereignty of the state.

Minute 13

Stallworth prepares himself for the covert operation. He fixes a wiretap to his shirt. As he does this alongside two white cops on the CPSD force, Stallworth begins to discuss hypothetical scenarios in which his cover might be blown as he's infiltrating the white supremacist gathering. What if they put a gun to his face, asks one of his colleagues? What if they offer him a joint? Stallworth's response is direct: he'll handle it. He'll deescalate when necessary, and be calm when things get out of control. One of the white cops seems to appreciate this strategy and says to Stallworth, "improvise—like jazz, like bebop." It's not entirely clear whether the cop intends to denigrate or compliment Stallworth. Either way, explaining the idea of improvisation through the genre of jazz and bebop as if, as a Black man, Stallworth can only understand concepts in musical terms, has a racist history. It bears echoes of the racist idea that Black people are naturally artistic, rather than philosophical. But the unexamined irony in the cop's remark is that there is a powerful conceptual link between jazz and improvisation as a way to think about political agency as such. Not because improvisation helps a police officer better conceptualize and carry out the work of the state—police work—but because it offers a model for thinking about citizenship. According to the novelist and cultural critic Ralph Ellison, the improvisatory nature of jazz is a central contribution of Black culture to American democracy. The ebbs and flows, making do with what's available—a blend between pragmatism and flexibility—is essential to living collectively, embracing freedom, and doing the necessary work to repair rifts in the fabric of existence. This improvisation is what American society needs but often is unwilling to embrace. Jazz and bebop musicians, for Ellison, are not just talented artists, but—in their collaborative and imaginative process—model an ethos of engagement, a way of being that resists orthodoxy and embraces the unknown. As Ellison writes, "Without the presence of the Negro American style, our jokes, tall tales, even our sports would be lacking in the sudden turns, shocks and changes of pace (all jazz-shaped) that serve to remind us that our world is ever unexplored . . . the real secret of the game is to make life swing."[8]

Minute 14

Stallworth arrives at the meeting space at night to hear Stokely Carmichael speak. He is surrounded by Black men and women in leather jackets, sunglasses, and berets—an iconic statement of revolutionary sensibility and political radicalism. Stallworth walks up to a Black woman, named Patrice Dumas (played by Laura Harrier) as she talks to several people, and introduces himself. They exchange pleasantries, and Dumas asks him if he has heard Kwame speak before. Stallworth is surprised—who is Kwame? Laughing, she explains that Carmichael has changed his name to Kwame Ture. The first thing that strikes the viewer in minute 14 is the shift in ambiance and mood. This meeting, of Black citizens, feels like home. The conversation is relaxed; warmth is presumed, and resentment is absent. Stallworth is among people who call him "brother" in an unironic sense (compared to how the white officers call him "soul brother"). In a world defined by white supremacy, these spaces, where

Black citizens feel at home, are indispensable. A Black counter-public serves the goal of revolutionary strategy. But it also fosters networks of intimacy, connection, and friendship. Social movements cannot subsist on strategy or tactics alone. They are successful only insofar as actors are nourished by the community they find themselves in. The practice of renaming, as evident in Kwame Ture's decision after he visits President Kwame Nkrumah in postcolonial Ghana, is a smaller-scale version of what happens in Black counter-publics. To change your name is to have agency over who you are, just as who you're surrounded by changes the meaning of what you feel might be possible.

Minute 15

As the conversation between Dumas and Stallworth unfolds, it becomes clear that Ture is invited to speak in Colorado Springs by the Black Student Union of Colorado College. Dumas, as it turns out, not only is part of the union but is its president. "May I skip the line since I'm talking to the president," Stallworth asks jokingly. "There's no cutting in line," she responds warmly but curtly. This brief exchange, seemingly innocuous and ordinary, actually paints a stark contrast between two alternative sensibilities. Stallworth's mode of engagement is based on flattery and humor (and, on some level, a patriarchal frame, which assumes traditional gender roles between men and women). Dumas's mode is primarily driven by the overarching idea of Black liberation—she treats Stallworth with the same democratic respect she treats everyone else, and, in doing this, refuses to bend those principles for the sake of adhering to a patriarchal image of womanhood as subservient. Dumas, in this sense, is thus the embodiment of the Black feminist tradition of organizing—a combination of Angela Davis and SNCC's inspiration Ella Baker. These are leaders and organizers who seek to model the kind of transformed world they want to inhabit. To achieve this world, there are no shortcuts. No skipping lines. The process is as integral as the result. As Baker once explained,

> On what basis do you seek to organize people? Do you start to try to organize them on the fact of what you think, or what they are first interested in? You start where the people are. Identification with people. There's always this problem in the minority group that's escalating up the ladder in this culture, I think. Those who have gotten some training and those who have gotten some material gains, it's always the problem of their not understanding the possibility of being divorced from those who are not in their social classification.[9]

Minute 16

"It is time for you to stop running away from being Black," says Ture (played by Corey Hawkins), as he steps up to the brightly lit podium, upon which is a sign with the inscription "Power." "You as the growing intellectuals of this country . . . you must define beauty for Black People. Now, that's Black Power." The camera cuts from Ture to Dumas, then to Stallworth, in an effort to establish the idea of Black multiplicity. Racism casts Black citizens as a simplified homogenous entity in opposition to whiteness—as if Blackness is a category that is clearly defined, constrained, contained, and obvious. The camera movement in minute 16, however, shatters this image, conveying the range and diversity of Black thought—Ture is the radical, Dumas is the radical feminist, and Stallworth is somewhere along the spectrum of a political liberal or traditionalist conservative. As political scientist Michael Dawson writes, "competing visions of freedom and the means to gain that freedom confronted one another within black communities . . . these visions . . . are ideological visions . . . [which] have been influential in shaping black political attitudes and practice."[10] In addition to shedding light on Black ideological diversity, the moving camera, floating from figure to figure, beautifully captures a productive sense of ambiguity and, maybe, imagines a transformed identity. The Black intellectual vanguard is imagined as a work in progress. We see how Ture's words inspire Dumas's feminism (even if that feminism offers a critical rejoinder to elements of masculine thought) and create space for Stallworth's discomfort about his apolitical worldview and, ultimately, a potential shift in thought. The shifting camera captures Stallworth's confusion—Ture's words and definitions, such as "Black beauty = Black Power," don't square with the white cops' characterization of Black identity. But this confusion gives way to new understanding—perhaps Black Power does resonate with his ultimate aspirations?

Minute 17

Ture continues his speech and begins to articulate the idea that Black beauty is a form of Black power. He meticulously describes the Black body—nose, hair, face, skin—to register its distinctiveness and dignity. Words and definitions matter. Language is crucial for the organization of social life. To put it in the words of philosopher J. L. Austin, it is possible to do things with words. Words have tangible effects in the world; they make things happen. And some words aren't just words; they give life to the reality that they aim to describe. Ture's verbal utterance, of unapologetically describing Black subjectivity in loving terms, has a profound performative impact on his audience. The camera moves back and forth between Ture and his Black audience—recalling what we might traditionally see at a political rally or during a church sermon—to establish the sense of recognition and affirmation that each member feels and experiences. The audience is listening intently, hanging on Ture's words, nodding in agreement, shouting "that's right!" and "yes." Politics, minute 17 demonstrates, is not only about acquiring power. Words have inherent political power. Language can be revolutionary and lead to existential change.

Minute 18

"White Tarzan used to beat up the Black native, and I would sit there, yelling, 'Kill the beasts! Kill them! Kill them! Kill them!'," Ture continues his speech. "But what I was saying was, 'Kill me'. Today, I want those chiefs to beat the hell out of Tarzan.... But it takes time to become free of the lies and their shaming effects on the Black mind." Colonialism, so argues the Black Martinican psychoanalyst and revolutionary Franz Fanon in his work, *Black Skin, White Masks* (1952), works not just through the colonization of political institutions and the built environment but through a certain kind and acute form of psychological domination. Insofar as the colonized's everyday life is governed by a necessary engagement with the attitudes and feelings of the colonizers, the sense of identity the colonized has is dependent on a social dialectic of power between them. When Fanon famously says, "Black is not a man," what he means is that Blackness in a colonized condition of white supremacy and is not a condition of freedom.

Whether constantly attempting to reckon with or discredit the colonizer's attitudes, fighting for survival, or grappling with feelings of domination—of shame and rage—Fanon insists that the space for Black autonomy is limited, if even existent. This pessimism, however, leads not to disengagement but to militant struggle. That's why Black revolution, or, as Fanon puts it, "decolonization," is the only response. Indeed, the very act of practicing the work to achieve revolution—of organizing, strategizing, criticizing, loving—is itself a necessary condition for unlearning colonialism. In the audience, at the back of the room, Stallworth begins to slowly recognize this, as he joins the audience in saying, "right, on." He surprises himself at what he is saying at his first political gathering.

Minute 19

"The vast majority of Negroes in this country, they live in captive communities. . . . Now we are being shot down like dogs in the streets," Ture continues, likening Black citizens in a racist system to animals without rights. Ture's metaphors have a specific resonance. To describe Black citizens as captive is to suggest that not only are they denied basic rights, but that they are held in a condition of bondage. Ture's formulation thus connects the 1970s—an era imagined to be post-racial, after the victories of the Civil Rights movement—to the era of enslavement, suggesting that racial progress is a myth. Life in captivity is the opposite of a white picket fence and an idyllic suburb—the myth of upward mobility Americans like to tell themselves. Life in captivity is defined by constraint, not openness; scarcity, not abundance. To describe Black citizens as being shot "like dogs" is to suggest that the foundational idea upon which representative government is legitimated in the United States—that it keeps its citizens safe and secure— is not only a myth, but that government does the opposite to nonwhite people—it actively destroys them. Ture's words connect to a tradition of Black political thought, which has long understood the power of narrative construction as a form of political critique—from Frederick Douglass discussing how enslaved people are treated as commodities on the open market of capitalism, to Huey Newton describing the "Black ghetto," as not dissimilar to a Nazi concentration camp. Even if not entirely accurate, metaphors like Ture's have a function: they sharpen the stakes and severity of one's claims and place their opponents on the defensive. Once one is placed in a position to explain how the metaphor is incorrect or misguided, they can no longer entirely dismiss the critique of dehumanization.

Minute 20

Ture begins to lead the crowd in a chant, after describing the Vietnam War as immoral and unworthy of Black support. "Hell no, we won't go!," he yells over and over again, raising his clenched fist, pumping it in the air emphatically. The crowd soon follows. Visual symbols are as significant as rhetoric in revolutionary movements. Ture's clenched fist is a symbol of Black Power, both as an emblem of solidarity and a force for resistance. To articulate a critique of the American state requires dispensing with patriotism and creating a contrast with the status quo. The image of the clenched fist, associated with Black Power, offers a vision of militancy and strength in the face of the unknown, just as it gives one a sense of their power. Feeling one's fingers wrapped in a ball, watching others doing the same, gives one a sense of their physical capacity—to do something, even if it's something as minor as raising a fist. One's hand—something so close and immediate to the body—anchors them and works as a form of labor to create a political statement.

Minute 21

"If I am not for myself, who will be? If I am for myself alone, who am I? If not now, when? If not you, who? All power to the people," concludes his speech. Compare Ture's speech (minutes 16–21) to that of the white supremacist,

Beauregard's, which begins the film (minutes 1–3). Both are clearly political speeches but of a completely different style and focus. In setting up the contrast between them, Lee critiques the false equivalences of political extremes (there are some who would say that Black radicalism, for instance, is the same as white nationalism, that talk of racial solidarity is dangerous, irrespective of the larger platform in which it emerges). But listening to Ture, the viewer understands the two extremes cannot, truly, be rendered equivalent. Black power is about Black self-love, of self-possession in a society where anti-Blackness is the norm; white nationalism, however, is about an aggressive and preemptive assault on Black people, on the very idea of plurality. Black radicalism is founded on embracing difference—and a democratic sensibility, a back and forth between leaders and the grassroots—white supremacy is structured around authoritarianism. Consider, for example, that Beauregard speaks directly to the viewer, never doubting the rectitude of his position, whereas Ture engages his audience, understanding that popular sovereignty is the lifeblood of any movement. Beauregard is gripped by paranoia (the imagined, mythical Black predator and criminal) whereas Ture speaks in historical and structural terms against racist cops, the war machine, and state-sanctioned violence. Ture aims to wield a sense of self-love and compassion in his audience, Beauregard aims to breed a sense of victimization and resentment. The two positions represent incommensurable views of reality.

Minute 22

After Ture concludes, Stallworth walks up to the podium. He asks Ture point-blank if a race war between white and Black is inevitable. "Arm yourself, brother," replies Ture, "because the revolution is coming." To be sure, there is strong historical evidence to suggest that the most effective antiracist movements—like the antislavery, antilynching, labor, Civil

Rights, and prison abolition—depend not on the threat of violence, but the threat of disruption. The general strike makes more of an impact than the gun; being organized is more effective than being armed. Yet, setting aside the ethical and strategic arguments for and against embracing a politics based on self-defense, what matters most here is that when Ture advises Stallworth about being ready for the revolution, he is articulating a unique political theory. Black power, from this perspective, is not driven by an antipathy toward white people, or by the belief that Black people are somehow morally or intellectually superior to all groups, but by a pragmatic account of politics. This pragmatic view of how to confront racism in minute 22 overturns critiques of Black Power (also directed against Malcolm X, James Farmer, Elaine Brown, and Charles Hamilton during their era), which imagine the movement to be founded in irrational hate. To the contrary, by arguing for Black self-defense, not only does Black Power challenge the myth of the liberal state (that the American state, according to the social contract, does fulfill its primary responsibility to protect all citizens), but it suggests that engaging with power—as it exists, not how we might want it to be—is what ought to be the task of Black politics. Notice the conditional structure of Malcolm X's argument in his famous address, "The Ballot or the Bullet":

> If you don't take an uncompromising stand, I don't mean go out and get violent; but at the same time you should never be nonviolent unless you run into some nonviolence. I'm nonviolent with those who are nonviolent with me. But when you drop that violence on me, then you've made me go insane, and I'm not responsible for what I do.[11]

Minute 23

"You won't believe what happened," says Dumas, as she arrives at a bar to meet up with Stallworth, after Ture finishes his speech. "Pigs pulled us over." The camera then quickly cuts to two white cops pulling over Ture and Dumas. One of the cops, Andy Landers, the one from Stallworth's precinct who calls him, "officer Toad," is visibly enjoying himself as he throws Dumas and Ture against their car, smiling. Landers mocks him: "I heard you was in town, Stokely." He then gives them an ultimatum: either you leave the town by morning, "or you'll all go to jail." The red, white, and blue of the police car siren is prominently flashing against his face, suggesting to us that nationalism, arbitrary power, and identity are deeply interwoven. To be in a position to execute and enforce the law of the state—as the police are—is a remarkable power. This power can create a sense of superiority that threatens democratic sovereignty. The state depends upon the police to exercise its will, to give it legitimacy, much more so than it depends on ordinary citizens—who, by virtue of their tacit consent or election seasons every two to four years—make their voice visible irregularly. Insofar as the police, however, organize the affairs of everyday life—controlling life in public—their power is less likely to be checked. When this happens, they are able to intensify already existing racial hierarchies. This is one of the reasons the Black Panthers saw as their task in the 1960s as "policing the police"—which is to say, recording, monitoring, and surveilling law enforcement in their Oakland neighborhood. In doing this, the Panthers sought to visualize a democratic check on sovereign power. With cops like Landers roaming the streets, such a strategy is understandable.

Minute 24

As Dumas relays this encounter to Stallworth, she is visibly frightened. The glass is shaking in her hand, she looks pensive and deeply uneasy. Stallworth invites her to dance with him, but even as Dumas is on the dance floor, she is still shaken. The trauma reverberates well past the encounter. Her fear is still alive in her body. Police brutality isn't only immoral; it has a debilitating effect on Black politics. The fact that Dumas knows she could be pulled over, that the police could target her and brutalize her—all while justifying their actions according to some malleable standard of probable cause or legal search and seizure—makes her wonder whether she should remain politically active or instead become invisible, assume a position of disengagement. As the political philosopher Lewis Gordon brilliantly explains in his recent work, *Fear of Black Consciousness* (2022), "Antiblack societies are therefore fundamentally antipolitical and antidemocratic—because they are devoted to blocking black people's access to citizenship. . . . This struggle reveals a feared truth of black empowerment: the fight against anti-black racism is ultimately a fight for democracy."[12] The meaning of anti-Blackness is apparent: Black political action has a cost, just like Black everyday life is a political choice. If Black citizens resist, they could always be punished, but even if they don't resist, they could always be marked by society or the state as unruly, dangerous, or criminal. The specter of the state always imagining Blackness as a threat to be confronted and managed makes it incredibly difficult for Black citizens to ever truly live in a state that is perpetually carefree, at ease—even as Dumas and Stallworth are dancing, trying to enjoy the moment, their minds are elsewhere, thinking about how their bodies might be marked by the state at any moment. Without warning. Instantly.

Minute 25

And yet, just as minute 24 puts forth a view that the cultural theorist Frank Wilderson calls "Afropessimism," which is to say, the idea that Black agency is forever constrained in a racist world, minute 25—an extended dance sequence between Dumas and Stallworth—provides an alternative view. The sense of hope, of possibility, is captured in the way their bodies are moving to the music and singing along to it, engaging in acts of self- and collective possession. Consider how their movement is supplemented by the lyrics of the song to which they are dancing—the 1972 R&B hit, "Too Late to Turn Back Now," by the Cornelius Brothers & Sister Rose. The joy. Freedom. Lack of constraint. Bodies in motion. Both the song and the dance express the Black novelist Ralph Ellison's view that even in conditions of domination there is always resistance, that all cultural artifacts (whether music or dance, in this case) express an underground, even if hidden, history of citizens refusing to be completely governed by political power. Black citizens, Ellison writes, "depend upon the validity of their own experience for an accurate picture of the reality which they seek to change . . . crucial to this view [is] a resistance to provocation," and "tenacious hold on the ideal of ultimate freedom."[13]

Minute 26

A recurring theme throughout *BlacKkKlansman* is the abrupt shift in mood. We are no longer in the lyrical space of the dance club. We are back at the police precinct. Stallworth is back at work, in uniform, being grilled by Bridges about the atmosphere of the Ture speech. "What was the room like?" Bridges asks. "Folks were hanging on his every word," Stallworth responds. Looking over the recorded transcript, Bridges tries to push Stallworth to confirm his established view that the Ture event was a clear example of subversive antigovernment activity—a prelude to insurrection. Stallworth pushes back. "Nobody in there was talking about [starting a revolution]. That wasn't the vibe. Everybody was cool." The conversation between Bridges and Stallworth isn't simply about facts—what happened? Who was there? But it is about the politics of truth. More specifically, it's a contest between positivistic knowledge and contextual knowledge. Bridges represents one epistemological framework—that of the logical positivist, as he paces the room, his eyes are glued to his notebook. He only cares about what the transcript says, the plain meaning of the words uttered. Stallworth, in contrast, is the contextualist, for whom meaning comes not from what someone only says, but what they mean, how they say it, and what they intend to accomplish with their words. These competing frameworks aren't just different philosophically. They can create markedly different outcomes. Imagine if Bridges's perspective wins out and context does not matter—this is the road toward mandatory minimums and Three Strikes Laws. Either someone is guilty of a crime or an inflammatory statement, or not. It's cut and dry. There is no room to consider history, motivation, or intention. Who wins in this battle? The answer is clear not only in US history, but visually. Bridges is the police chief; he is interrogating Stallworth. He, after all, is standing up, while Stallworth is sitting down.

Minute 27

Stallworth, nonetheless, presses his case against Bridges. Not only is Ture's talk of Black revolution "rhetoric," simply meant to inspire Black solidarity—there is nothing imminently dangerous about it, he explains—but the actions of the Colorado Springs Police Department (CSPD), he continues, are, in fact, more alarming. Shifting the focus of the conversation, Stallworth vividly describes to Bridges Dumas's experience of police brutality at the hands of Landers, to which Bridges asks: "are you sure you're not getting too chummy with her?" After Stallworth says he would never jeopardize an undercover case, Bridges sarcastically responds, "Let's just make sure it ain't under the cover of the sheets." Bridges's choice of words, "under the cover of the sheets," is not lost on the viewer—at this point, we are all probably wondering whether Bridges or other members of the CSPD force are secretly donning sheets themselves, which is to say, working as cops by day and riding with the Klan by night. This interpretation is not far-fetched. Many of the CSPD officers have already established themselves as racists. Perhaps what's more noteworthy, however, is not Bridges's sarcasm, but another white police officer, Flip (Philip) Zimmerman's reaction. Zimmerman (played by Adam Driver), Stallworth's coworker, sits beside Stallworth, and never comes to his aid to verify Stallworth's observations. This, despite the fact that Zimmerman listens to Ture's event firsthand (he is running the wiretap from a van parked outside) and, moreover, that Zimmerman is Jewish and thus knows all too well the anti-Semitic racism in the country. Zimmerman's silence is made worse by his laughter—he finds Bridges's "under the cover of the sheets" remark funny. A moment in which Black-Jewish solidarity could potentially undercut white supremacy and police brutality emerges as quickly as it dissipates. Zimmerman embraces his identity as a cop and as a white man, and, tragically, refuses antiracism.

Minute 28

Stallworth is back at his cubicle, carefully reading through the classified section of the local newspaper, when he comes across an advertisement for the local chapter of the Ku Klux Klan. Stallworth quickly dials the number and receives the answering service: "Hello, you have reached the Colorado Springs chapter of the Ku Klux Klan. Please leave a message. And God bless white America." What's so striking in minute 28 is how ordinary white supremacy is. We tend to imagine white supremacists as rabid racists, beyond the pale of normalcy—as outside the boundaries of decency and civility. Gritted teeth. Angry scowls. But the unsettling truth is that white supremacy has always tried to present itself as part of the mainstream. This is a conscious strategy—to normalize the movement, to make it less fringe and more palatable to the community. Notice how the answering machine message is respectful. Professional even. "Please," leave a message, the recording asks. The KKK is organized as a tidy local chapter, as if it's nothing more than an Elks club, bowling league, or rotary club. Nothing to see here, it says. We're just a regular civic organization with members who pay yearly dues.

Minute 29

The speed and intensity of the formation of white supremacy are startling. It forms fast, and unexpectedly. This is why it's a mistake to think of it as belonging to the past, of distant history. It is easy to recycle. The emotions and motivations that make one want to feel a sense of belonging—and the ease with which they can attach themselves to racism—make racism an ever-present possibility. Less than 10 seconds after placing the call, the camera zooms in on the telephone, which begins to ring. Stallworth is as shocked as the viewer. His eyes light up; he is not even able to finish a sip of his morning coffee. He's perplexed. A response already? Yes. The camera cuts to a shot of bespectacled Walter Breachway, president of "Organization," as he tells Stallworth. The speed of Walker's response leads us to think that he is never too far from the phone—as if waiting, on pins and needles, for a call to bring him to life, to give him a sense of purpose. Think about this contrast for a minute. Stallworth is just doing his job for which he gets paid—sitting by the phone to gather evidence for an investigation. For Walter, sitting by the phone, waiting for any call, is no job. It requires no payment. Practicing and recruiting for white supremacy is an experience that animates him. This disparity, minute 29 suggests, is precisely why white supremacy is never dead. It is always, to some extent, in a dormant condition, waiting to be activated by affects and circumstances. This is why it is so dangerous and cannot be treated lightly.

Minute 30

Walter asks Stallworth to tell him his "your story" in order to assess Stallworth's "fit" for the "Organization." Stallworth, pretending to be a rabid white supremacist, goes all in on the farce. He rages about Jews, Blacks, and Latinx people in a way that makes everyone in the office sitting next to Stallworth turn their heads, surprised that this is the strategy he is willing to take. One can imagine Stallworth using coded racist language—about a violent Black culture, Jewish success—but he doesn't. Instead, he calls Black people "baboons." Along with Stallworth's nasal accent (meant to affect middle-class white speech), this language is clearly over the top. But this is precisely the point. Without flinching, Walter eats up Stallworth's words and sounds. He loves how authentic Stallworth is. Stallworth, Walter says, is exactly the kind of man the organization is looking for. Walter and Stallworth both know Black people aren't "baboons," but the fact that they are able to say it out loud and share in this norm-breaking, this lie, makes them feel invincible, as if they are challenging the rules of reason or the very norms of humanity. Saying something preposterous is not a sideshow; it's the point in the quest for an exhilarating feeling of knowing that the racist is transgressing Enlightenment values. This gives Walter and Stallworth (acting as a white racist) a special bond, wrapped in conspiracy and malice. They viscerally feel the power of transgression, which, for them, is infinitely more enjoyable and exciting than the rules of civil society.

Minute 31

As if not to make the viewer feel too sure about the distinction between extreme racism (Walter and the Klan) and ordinary racism (the CSPD officers who we see throughout the film), the camera cuts to Stallworth trying to make his case to infiltrate the Klan to Chief Bridges. Bridges, without a second thought, immediately dismisses the idea. Why? Because, he says, whichever officer meets a Klansman in person (it can't be Stallworth) will sound different than Stallworth over the phone. Stallworth knows what Bridges is insinuating—that white speech and Black speech are different. Stallworth, feigning confusion, asks Bridges: is it that white people speak the "King's English," and Black people speak "jive?" Language is a central tool in the racist arsenal, so says Frantz Fanon in *Wretched of the Earth* (1961): "Violence in the colonies does not only have for its aim the keeping of these enslaved men at arm's length; it seeks to dehumanize them," he writes. "Everything will be done to wipe out their traditions, to substitute our language for theirs and to destroy their culture without giving them ours."[14] White colonizers demanded the nonwhite colonized to speak the colonizer's language, knowing that they have sovereign authority over what "proper" speech looks like. The colonized subject's speech can always be subject to interrogation, observation, critique, and diminishment. This, to degrade the colonized subject and reinstate the authority of the colonizer.

Minute 32

Minute 32 cuts to a police locker room, where we see Stallworth trying to convince Flip Zimmerman to represent him in person at Klan meetings. We understand why Stallworth would make such a demand, but we nonetheless wonder: is dishonesty or deception a sound basis from which to enact politics? For Italian political theorist Niccolo Machiavelli, the answer is yes. Masking and the performance of self, so says Machiavelli, are essential to political rule—the political ruler must always present themselves in ways to attract sympathy when necessary and fear when required. Deception, for Machiavelli, is thus a necessary virtue—one tool among many—that ought to be used strategically. As he writes in his pamphlet for political rule, *The Prince*, "in general men judge more with their eyes than with their hands," because "everyone sees what you appear to be, few perceive what you are."[15] In their conversation, Zimmerman and Stallworth theorize their presentation of self. What kind of mask to put on in front of the Klan? This raises the question of how exactly deception ought to be used and what ethics are necessary for confronting forms of political evil. Is truthfulness a virtue, or ought it be placed off its pedestal when confronting extreme movements?

Minute 33

In discussing the various available strategies for performing "whiteness" and "Blackness"—Stallworth has to, as he understands, "sound" white on the phone, and Zimmerman needs to "act" white in person by discussing his love of Christian talk radio and the Allman Brothers. One of the officers in the room overhearing the conversation confesses to Zimmerman that he "always wanted to be Black. All my heroes were Black guys. Willie Mays. Wilt the Stilt (Wilt Chamberlain) and OJ Simpson." Again, we see what *BlacKkKlansman* has been trying to dramatize for 32 minutes: race plays an outsized role in the white imagination. Blackness isn't just about one's skin color. It's about a larger cultural identity that, in this particular case, epitomizes the fantasy of cool. That Black citizens are grouped into an aesthetic category—of fashionable, hip—in the white mind speaks to the way racism, at its heart, is less about who Black people are, and more about what white people desire. To put this in psychoanalytic terms, the projection of white desires on the Black subject is a way for white people to keep these desires alive and real, without having to take responsibility for them. They can enjoy them from a distance, live them vicariously through Black citizens. For this reason, as James Baldwin writes in *The Fire Next Time* (1963), the only way for white citizens to fully address racism is to accept their own contradictions, rather than projecting them onto Black people they have never met. "The only way he can be released from the Negro's tyrannical power over him is to consent, in effect, to become black himself, to become part of that suffering and dancing country that he now watches wistfully from the heights of his lonely power."[16]

Minute 34

As the conversation between them continues, Zimmerman invokes a classic trope of white grievance since the 1960s—this is the critique of Black progress through the idea of unfairness. Echoing white citizens who railed against race-conscious programs in the late 1960s—affirmative action, school integration, busing—Zimmerman says it isn't fair that Stallworth gets to "act white," but that Zimmerman can't "act Black." In response, Stallworth gives Zimmerman an opportunity to "be Black" by having him read a script from a Black Power manifesto—so that their speech patterns and voices sound alike on the phone and in person. Zimmerman struggles to sound like Stallworth not because Stallworth is Black and Zimmerman is white but because Zimmerman is bad at imitation, and because his experiences don't align with the words on the page, which speak to the reality of Black domination. The white fantasy of being Black is dispelled at the very moment Zimmerman thinks he has access to it. Then, Zimmerman realizes the absurdity of the situation. The quest for Blackness is nothing but a distorted product of the white imagination.

Minute 35

After the back and forth between Stallworth and Zimmerman, Jimmy Creek (played by Michael Buscemi), a fellow white CSPD police officer in the locker room, jokingly tells Zimmerman that, now that Zimmerman officially sounds Black, the only thing left for him is to "lose the Jewish necklace." "Jimmy," Zimmerman corrects him, "it's not a Jewish necklace. It's a Star of David." There is a long and complex history of Black-Jewish politics in the United States. As Zimmerman's and Stallworth's quest to infiltrate the Klan reflects a potential moment of Black-Jewish solidarity against white supremacy, glimmers of the past resurface. Recall that US processes of racialization in the late nineteenth century, when waves of Eastern European Jews were arriving on US shores, rendered Jews nonwhite—in a way that created opportunities for racial solidarity between Jewish and Black citizens (the US labor movement, the Civil Rights movement, and the student movements of the 1960s all saw clear instances of this). At the same time, precisely because some (particularly European) Jewish citizens could pass as white to avoid anti-Black racism, the adoption of anti-Black racism among European Jews became one strategy to assimilate into US culture, and slowly weaponize whiteness to insulate themselves from racism and achieve greater social mobility. As Karen Brodkin explains, "Jews' and other white ethnics' upward mobility was the result of programs that allowed [them to] float on a rising economic tide. To African Americans, the government offered the cement boots of segregation, redlining, urban renewal, and discrimination."[17]

Minute 36

It is hard enough to decipher what it means to "act white." It's even more perplexing, however, to understand what it means to act like a white supremacist. Minute 36 tries to show us.

A prominent member of the Colorado Springs Klan, Felix Kendrickson (played by Jasper Pääkkönen) walks out of his truck, parked just outside what looks like a family diner. He has a mustache and slicked-back black hair. He is wearing a black-and-white flannel shirt and a jean jacket. Felix is looking both ways to make sure he's not being followed and gestures for Zimmerman to exit his car. Out from his Chevy pickup comes Zimmerman, with a trucker hat, red flannel shirt, and hands in his pocket. "Ron Stallworth?" asks Felix. "That's me." "Walter?" Felix asks in return. "Name's Felix." "Well, I was told I'd be meeting a Walter Breachway," Zimmerman responds. "Change of plans, Mac," says Felix. The terse and stilted conversation. The aggressive questioning. The cold, hostile exchange. Performing racism requires a certain commitment to masculinity—or, we could say, an understanding of manhood based on detachment, stoicism, rage, and impenetrability. For the racist to be taken seriously and to be welcomed into the fraternal order, they must prove their overt contempt for compassion, openness, and inclusivity. To be a racist isn't only to hold racist beliefs; it requires a certain presentation of self. Rigid. Vengeful. Angry. Toxic.

Minute 37

For "security" reasons, Felix tells Zimmerman that he needs to drive with him to an undisclosed location. At first, Zimmerman resists. Eventually, he gets into Felix's car. As they're driving, with country music playing in the background and the camera tracking their movements and exchanges, the mood shifts to something darker and more tense. We feel like we are no longer watching a comedy or social satire. Now we are seeing something from the pages of a slasher movie, where the unsuspecting, street-wise hitchhiker (Zimmerman) is being picked upon on a rainy night by a sadistic killer (Felix). The suspense is building. We're on the edge of our seats, watching to see if Zimmerman can hold up his performance of racism ("You for the white race, Ron?" asks Felix. "Hell, yea"). We can't help but notice how initiation into, or confirmation of, white supremacy is itself a form of captivity. Once Zimmerman asks to become a member of the Klan, he is no longer free. Now he is held hostage to the racist movement—for him to abandon it is to be deemed a race traitor. To not follow through on its violent demands is to be seen as a potential enemy, capable of disclosing its inner workings to the world outside. Before Zimmerman's initiation is even complete or he arrives at the undisclosed location, we feel dread. How can this end well?

Minute 38

The scene continues with Felix and Zimmerman in the car. Felix's instability begins to show after Zimmerman tells him it's an honor to meet someone with the Klan. Felix snaps at him, saying to never say that word: Klan. It's "The Organization." From now on, that's how Zimmerman must describe it. We all know what Zimmerman is saying, so why the obsession with linguistic details? The shift from calling it the "Klan" to the "Organization" reflects a long-standing trope of white supremacy. That is, to use language to masquerade racism. Recall how Jim Crow Segregationists formed "Citizens' Councils," whereas neo-Nazis today call themselves "white nationalists." The racist understands the power of language, especially in a liberal society where words hold sway over the popular imagination. The racist knows that a liberal society's commitment to pluralism requires that most viewpoints to be accepted as long as they don't explicitly incite violence, or create open conflict. To thrive in these societies without being ostracized requires generic language, or vague descriptors, which provide rhetorical cover for what is truly at stake. The more mainstream white supremacy sounds the more likely it survives in the public sphere.

Minute 39

Zimmerman arrives at the Organization's headquarters, which has a Confederate flag displayed out front. As he walks in, he sees Walter Breachway, who proudly wears a "white power" T-shirt and playing a game of pool. Walter tells him that he has been impressed with Stallworth's ideas based on their prior phone conversation. Moving past pleasantries, Walter gets down to business, saying, the Organization has been his salvation. It's a way for him to fight against Black people "taking over." Walter is obsessed with boundaries, and distinctions. Us versus them. This view is especially pronounced here, but it is also part of modern political thought, which relies on bounded communities—think the nation, or, at a smaller level, the political party or the labor union. Modern political thought worries about exceeding boundaries—whether an unruly protest or demonstration. This is why the state is so crucial. Boundlessness creates anxiety for modern citizens, so far-right groups learn to exploit this worry. They position themselves as the only ones capable of creating order, of policing those they demonize who are outside the boundaries of containment. Infestation. Mass migration. Irreversible demographic change. This is what must be averted, the right says. They alone could do it.

Minute 40

We might think there is a clear distinction between the rhetoric of everyday racism and full-fledged domestic terrorism. But the line is thinner than we would like to believe. Felix, a Klansman, expresses a common critique that we've long heard from the so-called moderate white majority—that political correctness, in the form of watching what we say about race, is unjust and unfair. "Watch your mouth. Don't say this, don't say that. Be nice. Hell, they ain't even colored no more. Negroes. Blacks. Afro-Americans now." Consider for a moment that this line of criticism is coming from a Klansman, not a white suburban Republican who is skeptical of affirmative action and doesn't like his words to be policed by the state. Felix treats racial inequality as a nonexistent problem and supposes that racial justice is itself an overrated project. Before long, the phrases of a conservative disgruntled, disaffected white citizen and a Klansman come to sound identical.

Minute 41

Felix gets close to Zimmerman and asks him quietly, with a sense of malice in his voice. "You undercover or something? You ask too many questions." This is not just Felix's paranoia that he's constantly being watched (even though, of course, we as viewers know that he is) it is also a general paranoia that pervades all members of the Klan. This is the idea that they are being infiltrated from within, corrupted from inside. For Felix and the Organization, the very act of asking questions, of engaging in the Enlightenment project of understanding and knowledge accumulation, is itself a threat, a sign that something is amiss. Compare this to minutes 16 through 21, when Ture is giving his speech. Ture's speech reflects a vision of radical skepticism—the critique of power, history, and social relations—whereas Felix and the Organization's is a state of forced enclosure. Fear and loathing encircle everything. They define the movement.

Minute 42

To Zimmerman's surprise, Walter takes him to another room and takes out a pile of paperwork. He then informs him that his initiation process into the Klan is nearly complete. The only thing left, however, is for Zimmerman to decide on membership options—"$10 for the year, $15 for the chapter." Robes and hoods are not included, Walter quips. "That's extra" Walter tells him, citing inflation. After this is sorted, Zimmerman can receive his membership card and participate in all the local and national programs. Here we are drawn into the boring logistics of maintaining white supremacy—fixed fee structures, laminated membership cards, tedious paperwork—in order to make clear that white supremacy isn't some spontaneous feeling, but requires organization. To bring us into these logistics is to demystify the aura of racism, as if it's some mystical, inaccessible thing. Racist groups are like any interest group, which depends on organization, sustained funding, and due-paying members. This is why abolishing racist feelings per se has never been at the forefront of antiracist struggles. The antiracists attack the resources that allow white supremacist organizations and political elites to flourish. They cannot survive without resources.

Minute 43

Felix continues to push Zimmerman—asking him if he isn't a Jew. According to racist theory, nothing could be more of an assault than to accuse the racist of belonging to the racial group he demonizes. This is an existential threat because racism itself rests on theories of immutable and hereditary identity. Of course, given the fact that genes and cultures are so widely hybridized, it's impossible to ever truly be pure, or, for that matter, to know for absolute certain what one's lineage or identity is. On the face of it, minute 43 is clearly trying to build suspense in the viewer by setting up the possibility that Felix recognizes that Zimmerman is, in fact, Jewish (we as viewers know that he is). But on a deeper level, however, we can't help but think, what if Felix or Walter—or any of the film's white supremacists—have Jewish (or, for that matter, Black) ancestors or blood that they are not aware of? Suppose that these racists somehow start to inadvertently develop attractions to or intimacies with those they racialize? The fetishization of purity and fundamentalist claims of racism put racists themselves in a trap. The very features they cannot control (their identities, and, sometimes, their feelings), according to racist theory, are precisely what animate the lingering fear that they themselves could always be race traitors—and thus represent the very thing they claim to loathe.

Minute 44

Cut to a new scene back in the CSPD precinct. "And exactly how much should we be worried about them?" asks the CSPD sergeant, turning to Zimmerman and Stallworth. Zimmerman, for his part, downplays the potential for Klan violence. They are mostly boasting about violence, they're not really serious. Stallworth emphatically disagrees with Zimmerman. Zimmerman's and the sergeant's initial skepticism (and, here we can infer this skepticism is also evident in the state) of taking the racist threat seriously reflects what the contemporary political philosopher Charles Mills argues in his book, *The Racial Contract* (1998). Aside from the classic social covenant known, from John Locke to Jean-Jacques Rousseau, as the social contract, there is a "racial contract," in which citizens of color's rights and freedoms are neglected, and those of white citizens are taken to be the only ones that truly carry moral and political weight. This racial contract, according to Mills, is what allows for governments to reconcile an obvious contradiction—how they can be at once committed to protecting all citizens' rights, but simultaneously deny the rights of racialized citizens. "But the peculiar contract," Mills writes,

> though based on the social contract tradition that has been central to Western political theory, is not a contract between everybody ("we the people" but between just the people who count, the people who really are people ("we the white people") ... the notion of a Racial Contract might be more revealing of the real character of the world we are living in, and the corresponding historical deficiencies of its normative theories and practices, than the raceless notions currently dominant in political theory.[18]

Minute 45

The next minute abruptly shifts visual and aesthetic registers, moving from the bureaucratic mechanisms of the police office to a candle-lit restaurant dinner between Dumas and Stallworth. As they're eating a candle-lit dinner and drinking wine, Patrice keeps talking politics—she's interested in how invested Stallworth is in the project of Black liberation, really? Patrice recounts a conversation she had with Ture earlier about the significance of Black women for the struggle and how her treatment at the hands of police gives her a unique experience regarding the intersectional nature of racial domination. Stallworth is visibly annoyed. Can't she just have a good time and not always talk politics? But this exchange raises the question: what is the meaning of a revolutionary life, exactly? Can revolutionaries enjoy dinner, and express intimacy, outside the demands of resistance" Are these activities impossible outside these confines? Must everything—including one's everyday life—be subject to political critique? Does the revolution demand total obedience, or something less stringent? At what point does a revolutionary lose their status and become incorporated into the very culture and society they criticize? Whatever the answer, the questions themselves are something revolutionaries grapple with and cannot avoid. To be a revolutionary demands not only acting with liberation on the mind but assessing one's commitments and contradictions at all times. This kind of self-examination is not easy, nor should it be. In fact, engaging in such examination is precisely what allows for the deconstruction and reconstruction of the self that can be part of a transformative movement. The conversation Patrice and Stallworth have is hard but necessary; that's the price of "being political."

Minute 46

We're still at the candle-lit dinner with Stallworth and Patrice. Patrice drops niceties. She asks Stallworth point-blank: "are you a cop?" Stallworth says no—he's a construction worker. He then goes on to change the subject, saying the most important thing is that he is in a relationship with Patrice, a strong, intelligent Black woman. Stallworth's deflection is part of a consistent theme in *BlacKkKlansman*; Stallworth is always undercover—with the Klan, he must disguise his Blackness, and with Patrice, he must cover up his police work. Zimmerman, too, is undercover—he downplays his Jewishness at work and hides his real work—as a cop—from the Klan. Social identities are implicated in webs of power that cannot be avoided. But how we make sense of, and what salience we place upon these identities, is still an open question. As much as Stallworth might only want to engage with Patrice outside the parameters of his social life as a cop, he still reproduces a structure of coercion of law enforcement, which disproportionately punishes and surveils Black citizens like Patrice. Zimmerman is infiltrating the Klan, but he is still a white police officer, whose presence in Black communities has a particular history and social function. What forces shape one's social identity? Is it simply their labor, or their position in social structures of race, gender, and sexuality? Is it possible to truly hide from these social identities, or must one take responsibility for them and work to reconstruct them in ways that are ethical?

Minute 47

Respectability is something with which the far-right has always had a tortured relationship. Racists understand the power of transgressing civil life—the shock value of uttering ideas beyond the pale. To scandalize is what animates the racist. At the same time, the racist desire to make racist ideas respectable and mainstream to make them more palatable reflects a preoccupation with upholding norms. Legalistic speech, tailored suits, button-down shirts. A headquarters. A charter. Mission statement. The conversation between Stallworth and the CSPD sergeant captures this—David Duke (played by Topher Grace), Grand Wizard of the KKK, so says the sergeant, always wants to be seen in a three-piece suit, and "never seen in a hood or robe in public." He goes by the title of "national director." He has clearly got his sights on a "higher office."

Minute 48

What is the value of didactic political education in art? This is a long-standing question in debates about the social responsibility of the artist. Should the artist stick to their craft, staying true to their creative vision despite political realities? Or must art be used to raise political consciousness? *BlacKkKlansman* insists that politics is unavoidable in art—after all, artistic choices depend on one's standpoint, which is informed by power—but that political art ought to be celebrated. The film's fictional dialogue aims to educate Americans about their society. In minute 48, the sergeant tells Stallworth (and, by extension, the audience) that Duke wants to politicize hate. Duke demonizes affirmative action, immigration, and higher taxation with the hope that one day this rhetoric can be sanitized and mainstreamed. Perhaps it could ultimately reach the White House. In response to this warning, Stallworth laughs, saying, "America would never elect somebody like David Duke president of the United States of America," as if to suggest that in the 1970s this sounds far-fetched. Of course, by 2018 when *BlacKkKlansman* was released, Americans know that this idea isn't far-fetched. 2018 is the second year in office of a US president, Donald Trump, who, in 2016 during his presidential run, refused to disavow the real David Duke, and who came to power explicitly endorsing white nationalism. Lee uses art to shed light on contemporary politics. His goal, however, is not to persuade citizens to shift their political leanings, but to provide an emotional and historical context for the world as they experience it. Few might have predicted the rise of Trump in 2016; but, if you look at that history closely (and the 47 minutes that came prior), perhaps there's a clearer line between the past and the present than you might think.

Minute 49

Next scene. Zimmerman arrives to Felix's house, where his wife, Connie Kendrickson (played by Ashlie Atkinson), welcomes him with open arms and a big smile. With a white apron on, she is busy preparing lunch for members of the Organization, who, led by Felix in his living room are debating the forthcoming race war, as they understand it. Notice for a moment the juxtaposition between Connie's warm embrace of Zimmerman as he enters her home and the violent conversations in the adjacent room. This jarring scene, the blending of love and death, might seem like a contradiction at first. But upon closer inspection, it is central to white supremacy. After viciously dehumanizing the racialized subject, the racist must double-down on attachments to their own identity. This attachment provides the racist the impetus to enact violence. Consider that in the late nineteenth century, love of "their community" was the justification for lynch mobs terrorizing Black people and white militias burning down Black neighborhoods. Even more disturbing were the lynching postcards, which captured hundreds—sometimes thousands—of white people, mobs smiling at a camera on the scene of the crime. These images would be circulated as mementos across the entire nation. Love and violence have motivated reactionaries for a long time. Remember the jarring argument made by US South Carolina senator Ben Tillman in 1907 before the US Senate. "We of the South have never recognized the right of the negro to govern white men, and we never will. We have never believed him to be equal to the white man, and we will not submit to his gratifying his lust on our wives and daughters without lynching him."[19]

Minute 50

"That'll be all, love you sweetie," says Felix, as Connie, bringing in cheese dip for lunch, tries to get into the conversation about white supremacist political strategy. Felix immediately shuts her down, stops her from uttering anything else, as she begins to talk about her own ideas about anti-Black racial violence. Race and gender are always linked. Writing in the late nineteenth century, Black feminist Ida B. Wells explained how white supremacy depended upon the practice of patriarchy. White terrorism was founded on the myth that Black men assaulted white women. "No one" would believe the "southern white man had a very chivalrous regard for the honor due the women of his own race or respect for the womanhood which circumstances placed in his power."[20] This myth became the way that white men were able to not only reinforce their social position. Insofar as white women, under white supremacy, were imagined and treated as passive, apolitical subjects, white men would see themselves as saviors in need of engaging in violence to "save" the nuclear family.

Minute 51

Felix brings Zimmerman into the basement, where he shows him a Remington shotgun. Felix calls the gun a "Jew killer." Walter—believing that things are getting out of hand, that Felix is becoming too aggressive with Zimmerman and is alienating him—asks Felix to stop. Felix is undeterred. His obsession with whether Zimmerman has "any Jew" in him runs deep. Felix demands that Zimmerman take a polygraph to prove his white purity. The lie detector, in this moment, is a symbol of scientific truth. Since racism and white supremacy always rely on specious, contrived facts about human identity and value, the racist, throughout history, turns to science to justify their project. From Carl Linnaeus's early attempts to categorize all the human races into a taxonomy to racial Darwinism, biological racism and eugenics, racists understand that science holds cultural currency as a form of truth and empirical validation. Obviously, the racist isn't terribly interested in engaging in rigorous experiments without bias—if they did this, their project would quickly collapse. Racism comes first—the science is used to justify preexisting assumptions and violence. But the racist appreciates science precisely when it serves their interests.

Minute 52

The tension builds as Felix, takes out his pistol, forces Zimmerman to sit down and take the lie detector test. As Felix tries to provoke Zimmerman, he proclaims that he thinks the

Holocaust is a "Jew conspiracy," that "Eight million Jews Killed?" "Concentration Camps," are fictions created to abet Jewish domination. "What's the proof? Never happened," he declares. This scene works in two ways. On the one hand, it creates suspense (will Felix discover Zimmerman's identity?). On the other hand, it subtly educates viewers in how to think like an antiracist. Associating Holocaust denialism with a figure like Felix helps dramatize the stakes for the viewer. You see the fine line between what we might call ordinary right-wing skepticism (think when someone says, slavery wasn't that bad, or structural racial inequality is not that big a problem) and hard-right epistemology (the Holocaust didn't happen, slavery was beneficial for enslaved people). Both are racist ideas, but the latter is much more vicious and menacing, as it takes on aggressive posture toward racialized subjects, claiming they fabricate the very pain they accuse racists of inflicting.

Minute 53

To deflect Felix's line of questioning, Zimmerman ups the ante on both toxic masculinity and anti-Semitism. "Cause I'd say the Holocaust is one of the most beautiful things I've ever seen," he defiantly tells Felix. "You have a whole race of leeches that you have to get rid of. So, what do you do? You starve them, you burn them, you get rid of them." That Zimmerman chooses this strategy—to be more aggressive, and confrontational, as a way to make Felix back down—is BlacKkKlansman's critique of liberal ideals of agreement. The liberal believes that the racist could be persuaded with more knowledge, better facts. This might lead them to abandon their heinous views. But the problem that the liberal refuses to recognize, or willfully overlooks, is that the racist will always find something devious, and conspiratorial about those they racialize. In the anti-Semitic imagination, for instance, either the Jew invented the Holocaust or the Jew is a leech who must be exterminated. In any case, the fact of the Holocaust itself (whether it happened or not) is less significant than the interpretation of its meaning and origins.

As Sartre explains, "AntiSemitism does not fall within the category of ideas protected by the right of free opinion. Indeed, it is something quite other than an idea. It is first of all a passion."[21]

Minute 54

Stallworth, listening to the interrogation, is parked in a car outside Felix's house. He knows he must create a distraction. As Felix tells Zimmerman to put the strap on his arm, Stallworth throws a rock through the window, which causes Connie, upstairs, to yell in alarm. Felix, along with Zimmerman, runs outside to chase a fleeing Stallworth. As the remaining members of the Klan run in pursuit, the camera reveals a lawn sign in front of Felix's house: "America, Love it or Leave it," is written on a US flag. Political philosophers have tried to redeem the concept of patriotism, as distinct from nationalism—insisting that patriotic civic virtue tied to ideas like liberty, equality, and constitutionalism—can be distinct from nationalism based on shared language or culture. The lawn sign in front of Felix's house reminds us just how dangerous any kind of national attachment could be—especially since it introduces a binary logic: "You're either with us or against us." This either/or admits of no ambiguity and provides a safe haven for racists who want to radicalize civic love to render it synonymous with racial identity and political belonging.

Minute 55

Zimmerman and Stallworth are back in the CPSD office. Now they are reprimanded by their acting sergeant for firing shots in the prior encounter with minute 54's encounter. Their superior, visibly furious and gesticulating wildly, worries that Chief Bridges won't tolerate this kind of behavior. He won't hesitate to have them all fired. "You dickheads are fucking with me, you're jerking my chain," the sergeant yells. Zimmerman and Stallworth can't suppress their laughter; it's funny how upset he is. Laughter, so says the essayist and novelist Ralph Ellison, is a way to reclaim self-hood, especially under conditions of terror and extreme psychic duress. By laughing about their terror, terrorized subjects are not consumed by it, find a way to distance themselves from the particular condition and horror of an event, and their humanity, their experience of being human.[22]

Minute 56

"You've been passing for a WASP. White Anglo-Saxon Protestant, cherry pie, hot dog, white boy," Stallworth confronts Zimmerman, as they go into the records office. This moment has been building over the course of the film, and now it reaches a boiling point. Stallworth will not tolerate Zimmerman's apathetic attitude toward racism. Zimmerman responds defensively. He believes Stallworth is taking the undercover operation too personally, like a "crusade," whereas, for him, it's just a "job." "Doesn't that hatred you've been hearing the Klan say, piss you off?" Stallworth asks, raising a political problem that has long dominated Black-Jewish politics (also see minute 35). By attempting to pass as white (changing their ethnic names, adopting casual, and not so casual, attitudes of anti-Black racism) and achieve greater upward mobility, some Jewish citizens abandoned the potential for a Black-Jewish antiracist alliance against white supremacy. The cost of this choice, however, was tragic. It diluted the ability for both groups to forcibly confront all forms of racism, which were brewing underneath the surface of US society.

Minute 57

Stallworth calls the Grand Wizard of the Klan, David Duke, to complain about not having yet received his Klan membership card. Duke picks up the phone. As he does this, he has to put on pause audio recordings of himself denouncing Jews and Blacks for destroying white civilization. Duke asks in a jovial tone—as if he is a customer service representative for a major company—"what can I do you for?" Immediately, the viewer is struck by just how young Duke looks, with his mustache and oversized suit (in 1972, when the historical Stallworth meets Duke, Duke is 22 years old). Upon closer inspection, Duke's youth is both comical and disturbing. That someone barely out of college can be a leader of a vicious white supremacist organization and command the imagination of older followers speaks to the way—contrary to popular narratives—not all young people are open-minded or liberal. Some youth become radical—but radical in ways that promote hierarchy. Moreover, their youth is precisely what makes them so appealing to their followers (think about the Charlottesville march in 2017, which featured hundreds of young people carrying tiki torches).

Minute 58

"Well, God bless white America," says Duke, as he hangs up the phone. "God bless, white America, sir," Stallworth replies. As this exchange occurs, the camera angle is tilted. Duke is on the left of the frame, while his desk and lighting are to the right. The viewer is thrown off-balance. There is a dizzying effect in terms of framing and narrative. The viewer is struck by the ease with which this conversation takes place, its awkward silences, its ritualized back-and-forth.

Minute 59

Zimmerman and Stallworth are preparing for the next round of surveillance, when Stallworth asks Zimmerman why, Landers, a white racist cop who had shot and killed a young Black man while on duty and assaulted Patrice Dumas, is still on the force. "Why do you guys tolerate this?" Stallworth wonders. "You want to be the guy who rats him out?" Zimmerman replies. Political theorist Hannah Arendt defines power as the ability to act in concert. Power is not just about force or strength. It's about having a network of willing support from below. "Power," she explains in *On Violence* (1970), is never the property of an individual; it belongs to a group and remains in existence only so long as the group keeps together. When we say of somebody that he is "in power" we actually refer to his being empowered by a certain number of people to act in their name. The moment the group, from which the power originated to begin with (potestas in populo, without a people or group there is no power), disappears, "his power" also vanishes.[23]

Police power, in Arendt's sense, comes from that fact that police officers are unwilling to dissent from the code of secrecy that binds them. Their collective silence keeps the institution afloat, with little checks and balance.

Minute 60

Zimmerman and members of the organization are out shooting in an empty field on the outskirts of town, and one of the members begins to complain about gay men visiting a local bar in Colorado Springs. "They're trying to colonize,"

says Walter, "You know, first they get their own bars, then they want equal treatment." The right imagines safe havens for the dispossessed and marginalized as sites of impending insurrection. Consider that, for instance, in the late 1960s, bars became a crucial space and symbol for gay liberation. Why? Because they provided a haven for marginalized citizens to organize and enact self and collective care in a homophobic society. The reactionary right, however, sees any attempts to accomplish this as dangerous intrusions, as themselves prequels for colonization. Because the reactionary does not believe in equality or holds the value in low esteem (below, for instance, authority, tradition, or hierarchy) attempts at achieving equality—no matter how limited—are treated with contempt, if not organized around an existential fear. If equality is no longer in your political vocabulary, everything is viewed as a war of all against all.

Minute 61

As Zimmerman and Organization members leave the field, the camera slowly pans to the barren landscape. Beyond the overgrown fields, withering away without sunlight, we see Stallworth, walking slowly into the frame with a brown leather jacket and dark orange button-down shirt, surveying the empty shells littering the field, with camera in hand. He picks one up, and examines it carefully and slowly. Minute 61 crystallizes a theme the film has been developing throughout, which reverses expectations in the racist imaginary. Stallworth is, in fact, a Black hero on the hunt against white racists. Positioning Stallworth as the central protagonist gives the viewer a vision of Black complexity, which, as overturns the simplified image of Blackness in the white mind, vacillating between the archetype of a generous and deferential sidekick to the unruly criminal.

Minute 62

Stallworth walks over to the site of the shooting range and sees for the first time what we also now see—the Klan's shooting drills are being practiced on what appear to be metallic silhouettes of Black men in the act of running. The camera stays on this image for 15 seconds to let us appreciate the ferocity of the racist imagination. The viewer wonders: what is the labor that goes into producing this? How much time did it take to produce these silhouettes? Under what conditions? With what end in mind? White supremacy requires labor. It takes time, effort, and energy. To uphold racism, one must be invested in creating and recreating it over and over again. It cannot just be an unconscious fact or based on ignorance. White supremacy, like this metallic silhouette, is a clear-cut choice.

Minute 63

The camera pans across a lush landscape, in which we see Patrice and Stallworth walking along a narrow bridge overlooking a scenic river. Stallworth, in a moment of vulnerability, asks Patrice if she, deep down, believes it's possible for a Black cop to change the system from inside. Patrice doesn't think so. She says, "You can't change things from the inside. It's a racist system. . . . We fight for what Black people really need. Black liberation." The conversation between Patrice and Stallworth echoes a core debate within Black political thought from its inception: what is the efficacy of pragmatism against that of radicalism? Recall Frederick Douglass's attempts to negotiate with Republicans to include Black troops in the Union army during the Civil War, to Martin Luther King, Jr.'s decision to engage with the Democratic Party in the 1960s in an effort to pass Civil Rights legislation. Working from within the system, Black pragmatists argue, creates results. The critique of pragmatism comes from Black radicalism—socialists like

Hubert Harrison, Marxists like Hosea Hudson, Black Power advocates like Malcolm X, anarchists like Lucy Parsons, nationalists like Marcus Garvey—which argues that racist power must be toppled and dismantled by any means necessary. If it means working outside the system, then it's necessary.

Minute 64

Referencing Black sociologist W. E. B. Du Bois's famous line about "double-consciousness" of being both Black and American, from his classic book of essays *The Souls of Black Folk* (1903), Patrice tells Stallworth that the Black condition is defined by "two warring ideals inside one dark body." But "we shouldn't have a war going on inside ourselves. We should just be Black," Patrice continues. For Du Bois, this existential conflict of double-consciousness within the Black self is both a descriptive account of Blackness as a specifically modern experience—the focus on identity, the quest for universals, the struggle against time. At the same time, double-consciousness is Du Bois's indictment of that modern society itself. In articulating the very existence of such a phenomenon, Du Bois identifies anti-Black attitudes in a modern society that is ostensibly committed to equality, rights, and freedom for all. That Black citizens don't get to enjoy these liberal values reflects a fundamental contradiction at the heart of a society that calls itself democratic.[24]

Minute 65

A dim apartment hallway. There we see Felix knocking on a door, waiting for a response. To our surprise, the apartment at which he is standing is Stallworth's. Stallworth opens the door, with Patrice alongside him. His smile turns into a state of shock. "Wrong address," says Felix with a smile. "Sorry to bother you, sir. Have a good night." This is the first time in the film that we see Felix interact with a Black man, in the flesh. What's remarkable, we realize, is how easily Felix can adopt the veneer of civility toward Stallworth, all while harboring deep and violent hostility. Viewed from a historical perspective, this is neither new nor especially surprising. Civility has been adopted by racists in precisely this way. From slaveholders who claim that they are invested in the well-being of the enslaved to Jim Crow mobs that proclaim respect for Civil Rights protestors, civility has long been a way for racists to protect themselves from critique. Presenting themselves as civil allows the racist to deflect attention away from the violent ends of their desires and objectives.

Minute 66

Zimmerman arrives at Walter's apartment, where Felix confronts him: "you got a twin?" Zimmerman is surprised, but Felix presses on, telling him that he visited his apartment to find Stallworth there. It's a mistake, Zimmerman replies emphatically. Impossible. His number is unlisted. This recurring theme of Felix's obsession with Zimmerman's identity isn't only a foundational plot point meant to build up a sense of tension throughout the film. The viewer, through 66 minutes of the film, feels Felix's obsession viscerally. What kind of inner life must one have to live in this way? What effect does it have on all aspects of one's self? Felix's obsession raises the thesis that the process of adopting racism has a devastating psychological impact on the racist, infusing all aspects of their lives, and dominating their behaviors. Felix's anti-Semitism becomes who he is and what he does. This is a horrifying condition. A condition no subject would want to embody.

Minute 67

Zimmerman and Stallworth are back in the office, discussing the key figures in their investigation so far—Felix, Walter,

Connie, and Duke. Pictures and names are placed on a whiteboard to track to the available evidence. This framework is meant to remind the viewer of the main criminals in the film. Despite the film's comedic representation of white supremacy (it is uncouth, unfocused, easily infiltrated)—it is nonetheless a lethal enterprise that ought to be treated seriously as a political and existential threat. One could laugh at racism, but laughter cannot be the primary response.

Minute 68

The camera shifts to a close-up of Zimmerman, who confesses something he has not told Stallworth before. "I'm Jewish, yes," he tells Stallworth, "but I wasn't raised to be. It wasn't part of my life. I never thought much about being Jewish. Nobody around me was Jewish . . . I was just another white kid. I never thought about it much. Now I'm thinking about it all the time." Zimmerman is honest, self-critical, and attentive to his personal history, which intersects with a wider social history. He is open, rather than defensive. Receptive, rather than guarded. Zimmerman, in this sense, models the kind of critical recognition *BlacKkKlansman* wishes white citizens would undertake—an awareness of the psychic and political benefits of whiteness, and a refusal to accept it.

Minute 69

"Is that passing? Well, then I have been passing," Zimmerman says to Stallworth, as he tosses his Klan membership card to Stallworth. "I don't want that," he says, as he sighs and walks away out of the frame. Zimmerman's recognition of his desire to flee to whiteness and the ease with which he was able to deny the salience of racism in US society is precisely what, on an existential level, theorists of race believe to be essential for restorative justice. But one might nonetheless wonder: is this recognition, of the wage of whiteness, adequate to address histories of violence? What exactly ought to be the value placed on recognition over redistribution? For political theorist Nancy Fraser, there is a disturbing trend in contemporary politics, "questions of recognition are serving less to supplement, complicate and enrich redistributive struggles than to marginalize, eclipse and displace them . . . this [is] *the problem of displacement.*"[25]

Minute 70

Zimmerman and Ivanhoe are sitting in a car at night, as another member of the Klan, Ivanhoe (played by Paul Walter Hauser), tells him about Klan strategies of cross-burning. "Yeah, you soak the wood in kerosene. And light a cig on a pack of matches. It kind of buys you some time to get the fuck out before the cross catches fire. . . . It's great. It's a real bonfire. You can see it from miles away, you know? Good visibility," Ivanhoe says. Sensational deeds are often deployed by political movements to bring attention to their cause. The symbolism of the deed, however, is as important as anything else. The burning cross places racists in a discursive framework of religiosity while at the same time engages in a profane desecration of sacred symbolism. The participation in and transgression of religion is the point. The racist wants to be within the "law" (as a religious person, a good Christian, decent family man) but also outside, sovereign and beyond religion. He is destroying the cross, watching it burn in flames. In doing this, he means to suggest that he, and his movement, is more powerful than religious institutions and doctrines.

Minute 71

As Zimmerman and Ivanhoe continue their conversation, they listen to a recording of David Duke: "this program," he says,

58 BLACKKKLANSMAN

"dares to love white people, white heritage, and white freedom. This program also dares to expose Jewish supremacism and the criminal banking establishment.... They're ethnically cleansing our people." The racist consciously mobilizes the very human rights language that was once meant to excise him from the public sphere. In *Origins of Totalitarianism* (1951), Hannah Arendt famously remarked that the Nazi concentration camps made clear that the discourse of human rights was nothing in the face of arbitrary power. Minute 71 inverts this idea, suggesting that the discourse of human rights is a powerful rhetorical way to promote sovereign power. Recall that the institutionalized response to ethnic cleansing came about in the post–Second World War era with the Universal Declaration of Human Rights of 1948. And yet the racist, Duke, claims that white people are, in fact, the true victims of ethnic cleansing. Against Arendt, the racist does not simply abandon human rights discourse; indeed, they are aware that insofar as human rights discourse is now mainstream, the language of politics, business, society—the racist must position themselves as the great champion of human rights in order to promote his reactionary objectives.

Minute 72

The Duke audio recording continues in the background. Except now the scene changes and Felix is surveilling Patrice, as she exits her house and gets into her red car, a Volkswagen Beetle. As Felix watches Patrice, Duke's voice echoes ominously in the background:

The only thing we hear today from politicians ... I love black people ... and of course every politician has to talk and genuflect to the real rulers of our society and say, I want to thank the Jewish people. I love the Jewish people. The Jewish people are always our friends, no matter what they do, no matter how much they destroy this country.

As rational actors, politicians don't love anyone; they simply act in ways to promote their self-interested pursuits to remain in power. But by transforming a rational constituent relationship into one that is being manipulated by a select few, the racist aims to create feelings of disgust around the political process as such. By transforming the image of a politician as too weak and hostage to hidden Jewish desires, the racist simultaneously reinforces racism and denigrates the potential liberal political process—here, the electoral process—that potentially poses an existential threat to them.

Minute 73

"In the sense, they're like a good dog," says Stallworth to Duke over the phone, who nods approvingly, "They get real close to you, and as soon as you lose them, it just breaks your heart." Metaphors of animality abound in the racist imagination. But Stallworth, in parodying white supremacy, homes in on a crucial theoretical point. The racist invents the racialized subject, and in so doing, requires that subject's existence to make sense of themselves. The meaning and identity of whiteness, in other words, is inextricably linked with its opposite—that of Blackness. This is why Stallworth's remark— and Duke's agreement—captures more truth than Duke would like to admit. The racist needs the racialized subject to know themselves; once that subject escapes the racist definition, the racist is at a loss.

Minute 74

Stallworth tells an apocryphal story about a Black boy named "Butter Biscuit," who the young Stallworth once played with, but who his father told him to avoid because he was Black. "My father was a true American," Stallworth tells Duke, "he taught me what was right." We have seen a variation of this idea between racism and Americanness before in the film (minutes 54 and 64). But minute 74 explicitly foregrounds the connection between nation, race, and manhood. All three concepts are based on a notion of inheritance, on a passing down of traditions and cultures. All are made together, which is to say constructed and invented—they are not natural. And all are mutually reinforcing and intertwined. Race, nationhood, and manhood require narratives of difference, hierarchy, and enclosure.

Minute 75

The following scene cuts to Patrice in an extravagant library, poring over microfilm of what appear to be newspaper clippings about lynchings of Black people. How can one be patriotic when American history is violent and bloody? In the words of James Baldwin, it is filled with the "corpses of his [Black] ancestors?"[26] Lynching and racial violence were not a problem restricted to the South—but was common throughout the country. One of the clippings that Patrice examines, in particular, has a striking resemblance to a historical lynching that took place in Duluth, Minnesota, on June 15, 1920, when three Black laborers working for a traveling circus—falsely accused of raping a white woman—were dragged out of a county jail by a mob (estimates range between 1,000 and 5,000), beaten, and murdered. This is not Mississippi. This is Minnesota.

Minute 76

Walter calls Stallworth to ask him to be the Organization's new leader because he's more articulate and possesses better leadership qualities than Felix, who Walter describes as a "loose canon." All political organizations encounter power struggles and tension. What makes fascist and authoritarian organizations less likely to survive is that struggle and unpredictability are central to their ideology. As Hannah Arendt writes, the terror of totalitarianism is based on the fact that it is constantly changing and refining the instruments of terror, that those who enact the terror need to lose sight of their humanity, need to be willing executioners of the sovereign's command. As she writes, "Terror becomes total when it becomes independent of all opposition; it rules supreme when nobody any longer stands in its way. If lawfulness is the essence of non-tyrannical government and law-lessness is the essence of tyranny, then terror is the essence of totalitarian domination."[27] Felix's unpredictability is what makes him such a loyal follower of the Klan—an asset to the organization— but also what makes him a permanent threat to break its rules, violate its codes, and jeopardize its existence.

Minute 77

"Aren't you ever concerned," Stallworth asks Duke about a Black person calling you, "pretending to be white?" "No," responds Duke. "I can always tell when I'm talking to a Negro." Stallworth answers the question that many viewers have been asking themselves for the past 77 minutes: at what point will Duke become aware of the ruse that Stallworth and Zimmerman are playing on him? Duke's confidence in knowing he is not being tricked (even though we know he is) captures a larger point about the racist: the absurd sense of total confidence. The racist worldview is so steeped in delusion, inconsistency, myth, and falsehood that confidence is what keeps it together.

Minute 78

"I can tell that you are," Duke pauses. Stallworth is on edge, wondering if he's been discovered, "a pure Aryan white man from the way you pronounce certain words." Language, one of the most elastic and culturally hybridized and evolving modes of communication, has always been singled out for special consideration by the racist. On the face of it, there is something absurd about this fascination. Given the variety in speech, dialect, and language, how could any pronunciation of words be intrinsically connected to racial identity?

In the metaphysics of racism, there is a connection between word and essence. The way one utters their words, inflects their letters and sounds, is proof of some larger truth about their identity.

Minute 79

"Wow. You are so white. Thank you for teaching me this lesson," Stallworth responds with a sense of disbelief and visible irritation, "If you had not brought it to my attention, I wouldn't have noticed the difference between how we talk and how Negroes talk." Ralph Ellison famously reminded readers that much of American culture, and therefore, the English language is hybridized. The violent process of racial enslavement and colonization created a process through which Black culture became a central part of American culture. "There was a modification of language necessary to communicate with the slaves and with the people who come from other parts of Europe. All of these created a tension which in turn created what we call the vernacular style."[28]

Minute 80

Felix brings Zimmerman to an emergency meeting in his basement. There we see Klansmen gather in front of a stockpile of artillery and weapons. "We're gonna need your good shoot come next Sunday," says Felix to Zimmerman. "The war is gonna come to us." The scene evokes both a ritual of initiation and a religious experience (all of them are worshiping at the altar of the weapons, admiring them as if they are sacred objects). Objects of violence are not just means to an end; in the fascist imagination, they are an end in themselves, to be celebrated. So when we talk about "culture wars," it is critical to remember that culture can sometimes be much more than the basis for one's policy preferences. The policy is a fundamental extension of identity. No wonder the far-right refuses to discuss the policy of gun control. For them, private ownership of the gun is an extension of one's self, one's community, and the very essence of what it means to be a citizen.

Minute 81

"Honey, do you ever have second thoughts about killing them?" Connie asks Felix while they're lying in bed at night and as Felix rubs her hair back gently. "It's just becoming so real," Connie continues. "I always thought it would be like a dream." This is the only moment in *BlacKkKlansman* where the white supremacist undergoes any kind of moral reflection about their actions and briefly considers the immorality of anti-Black racist violence. What's striking, however, is that this brief instance of ethical awakening reveals how racism, fundamentally, relies upon a fantasy. Not only the fantasy of a pure return to nonexistent origins—of racial purity, of racial restoration—but of the belief that rhetorical violence can be firmly severed from real violence. The racist, in language and culture, prepares for the annihilation of his imagined racialized enemies. But this preparation is never enough, especially given the racist's investment in authenticity and true meaning. Once that conflict between rhetoric and deed comes into ultimate conflict, and becomes irresolvable, a crisis emerges. The racist is forced to consider the goals, desires and meaning of their identity, and the extent of their commitments. This moment of crisis, however, is also an opportunity for the antiracist. It is at this point when the antiracist can force the tension into the open not only for the racist but for all of society to see, so that citizens can determine whether they should ever tolerate racism in their midst. The purpose of antiracist action, according to Martin Luther King, Jr., is to

> create such a crisis and foster such a tension that a community which has constantly refused to negotiate is forced to confront the issue. It seeks so to dramatize the issue that it can no longer be ignored. . . . Just as Socrates felt that it was necessary to create a tension in the mind so that individuals could rise from the bondage of myths and half-truths to the unfettered realm of creative analysis and objective appraisal, so must we see the need for nonviolent gadflies to create the kind of tension in society that will help men rise from the dark depths of prejudice and racism to the majestic heights of understanding and brotherhood.[29]

Minute 82

"Thank you for bringing me into your life," Connie says, smiling, after Felix reassures her of the necessity of murdering Black people. "For loving me like you do. For giving me a purpose, giving me direction." Felix stares off into the distance, dreaming about the revolutionary potential of his deeds, "This could be the next Boston Tea Party," he says, eyes gleaming. The mixture of melodrama and self-delusion is, on one level, comical. We know that whatever the Klan does—no matter how violent—it will amount to nothing more than a criminal act. There will be nothing transformative about it. But this is not what the Klansman believes; to become invested in the movement, they need a higher purpose that renders politics into a spiritual act. This is where the comedy turns into deep terror. Politics, in other words, becomes dependent upon a transcendent theology unto itself that allows it to escape the rational. We are no longer in the realm of means and ends—we are in the realm of religious necessity. Once white supremacy assumes this form, finding common ground becomes impossible. The only way to confront it is through creating a counter-hegemonic force—or to use Hannah Arendt's idea of "power"—that can subdue it.

Minute 83

Under a bridge, in an abandoned area of town, Stallworth meets with a man in a gray suit, who we presume to be working with the FBI (Federal Bureau of Investigation). Two of the men affiliated with the Klan—whose names we don't know, but we see on the periphery of some scenes—as it turns out, work for NORAD (North American Aerospace Defense Command), a government organization between the United States and Canada, which, until 1981, was responsible for air sovereignty. The FBI agent tells Stallworth that these men aren't undercover; in fact, they are drawn to racist ideas. The affinity between sporadic right-wing violence and the organized violence of the state makes sense. The two share not only a commitment to cohesion and hierarchical structure but also means-justify-the-ends thinking. In *Politics as a Vocation* (1918), political scientist Max Weber famously defined a state as the entity capable of monopolizing the use of force in a given geographic territory. In couching war as necessary for the preservation of sovereignty (the sovereignty of the nation or racial identity), both the state and the extremist organization, in their own way, imagine violence to be central to the practice of politics itself. In their interpretation, war and politics are inescapably linked, mutually reinforcing, and part of the very field of strategic action.

Minute 84

Stallworth warns Patrice to avoid going to the Black Student Union demonstration that is taking place later that afternoon, of which she's the acting president. He has inside information, he tells her, about a Klan attack and reveals knowledge about an active CSPD investigation. Patrice, confused, asks how it's possible that he knows all this. Is he a pig? On first glance, Stallworth's desire to protect Patrice from harm reflects something positive. On the other hand, we have seen this narrative before in *BlacKkKlansman*: that is, the image of (white) men saving (white) women. We know that this patriarchal image fuels anti-Black violence. With this in mind, Patrice's confrontational approach to Stallworth represents an alternative Black feminist political theory. Patrice, for her part, is less invested in whether Stallworth's individual actions (or his police work) successfully protect her. She is more concerned with whether his role as an instrument of the state is to perpetuate institutions of violence against Black people. Patrice, therefore, enacts what civic republicans deem a virtue of politics: to place concerns of the public good over personal-particular interests.

Minute 85

"No," Stallworth answers. "I'm an undercover detective. I'm investigating the Klan." Understandably, Patrice is startled and confused. She asks Stallworth how long he has been lying to her. Is Ron his real name? Is he "for the revolution and liberation of Black people?" Stallworth pauses, then responds: "I'm an undercover detective for the Colorado Springs Police." Patrice shakes her head in disbelief and storms off into the crowd of students at the protest. To echo minute 84, the sense of personal betrayal that Patrice feels in being deceived is less significant than her outrage over Stallworth's social role. In politics, we are often told to focus on the individual heart and soul of people, their inner lives, who they are as people— rather than the institutions that their labor perpetuates. And yet, individual character is often a powerful and effective way to silence critique—the cop engaged in police brutality says he's a good person, the general who goes to war says that, in his heart of hearts, he is honorable. Patrice refuses this logic and does not believe Stallworth's individual character is a way to exonerate him for his structural position as a cop.

Minute 86

Stallworth is back in the investigation room with Zimmerman, where he tells him that he's told Patrice the truth about his police work. Zimmerman is outraged that Stallworth tells Patrice the truth, that he crosses the line between work and his intimate life, and that he threatens to derail an investigation that they had been working on for months. "Hate to break that blue wall of silence," Stallworth responds derisively to Zimmerman's anger. Zimmerman is hell-bent on continuing the investigation, avoiding any complicating factors that might cause him to feel ambivalence about the assignment. Zimmerman is motivated by duty, by doing his job, in a way that raises troubling parallels with the Klan. Zimmerman's desire to "just do his job," Hannah Arendt calls the "problem of thoughtlessness," which is to say, the blind obedience toward authority. Upon closer inspection, Zimmerman's singular focus on following orders, or doing his job faithfully, is not too dissimilar from Walter's or Felix's conviction in following the objectives of the Klan. Irrespective of these strikingly different motivations and objectives, citizens who abandon ethical inquiry and critical judgment are complicit in perpetuating injustice.

Minute 87

Chief Bridges interrupts a conversation between Stallworth and Zimmerman. He tells Stallworth that he needs to be temporarily reassigned from the investigation to pursue another assignment. There are credible threats to David Duke's life (Duke is coming into Colorado Springs the following week) and the CSPD needs to provide him with a security detail. Stallworth, Bridges asserts, will be Duke's police escort. In response, Stallworth is visibly upset, knowing that he and Duke have spoken numerous times over the phone. "Put aside your personal politics," Bridges says. Compare Bridges's concept of the personal versus political to Patrice's (see minutes 84 and 85). Unlike Patrice, Bridges urges Stallworth to abandon the integrity of his antiracist commitments for the sake of deferring to the demands of the institution (law enforcement) for which he works—an institution that is not driven primarily by self-perpetuation (responding to budgetary limits or the chain of command). Patrice demands Stallworth to not hide behind his personal commitments to thoughtlessly perpetuate unjust institutions, while Bridges demands Stallworth perpetuates unjust institutions and not allow his internal ethical or critical considerations to neutralize that process.

Minute 88

The camera shifts to Felix's basement, where Connie, his wife, is being guided by a man we have not encountered before on how to place and donate a purse full of explosive C-4. Felix and other Klansmen watch on. Connie is visibly excited but also anxious and somber. Her eyes track the man's every move as he details the plan and he shows her how to flip the remote control switch to detonate the device. We have seen this dark basement before throughout the film, but now this space feels more claustrophobic and enclosed. Suffocating. Connie tries to muster a sense of purpose and joy, but she feels entrapped. White supremacy, as a system, has closed off her possibilities for freedom and enlisted her in its violent fantasies from which she cannot escape. As her eyes open wide, we feel a sense of ambivalence and thus, a sense of possibility—maybe she might break free (in resonances with minute 82)? But the enclosure and darkness of the room, like white supremacy, is too comforting. She is entrapped. To flee is to risk the threat of violence.

Minute 89

Stallworth arrives just outside a hotel, which is surrounded by Klansmen and supporters of David Duke (Zimmerman, we notice, is also there among them). As Duke walks down the stairs and exits the building, Stallworth swiftly approaches him—to the surprise of the bystanders—and announces to Duke that, as a CSPD police officer, he will be providing him security. Duke's shock is palpable, but so too is the viewer's. What exactly are the limits of liberalism, we wonder, in a society that relies upon pluralism? What happens when pluralism is recruited to give cover to violent ideology, to safeguard white supremacy? What happens when pluralism is used to dominate citizens who are marginalized, whose rights are at risk, and whose rights pluralism is meant to protect in the first place? Is this a necessary concession? Something that upholds the principle of equality? Is it fair?

Minute 90

"Mr. Duke, I don't agree with your philosophies," says Stallworth, "However, I'm a professional, so I will do everything within my means and beyond to make sure you're safe." "Okay," Duke nods, "I appreciate your professionalism." There is a wide gap between Duke's appreciation, on the one hand, and Stallworth's restraint, on the other hand. This gap speaks to the limits of Black freedom under liberalism. Black citizens, so argues a critical strain in Black political thought, are expected to live in a state of anxiety, to tolerate that liminal state, as a necessary condition of citizenship. As long as white violence is imminent, or cannot be proved to be so, the Black citizen must show professionalism, whereas the white racist can operate with impunity as long as they carefully walk the line between their racist words and deeds and escape the grasp of the juridical system.

Minute 91

A motorcade, buttressed by white bikers in leather jackets and sunglasses, protects Duke's Cadillac limousine as it moves slowly through downtown Colorado Springs, along its narrow, circuitous roads, and arrives at Pike's Lodge Banquet Hall at the Colorado Tejon hotel. The motorcade loops like a snake, flexible and spiraling to contain Duke. The imagery is striking and philosophically rich. Duke might be the head of the organization, but it is the grassroots that protect him, give him defense. The bikers are part of a long iconography of right-wing terror—from the Night Riders to lynch mobs to Citizen Councils. And yet, precisely because the bikers are not an army—their power rests on the theatrics of intimidation, not an arsenal of advanced warfare—they cannot compete with the force of the state.

Minute 92

Stallworth stands to the side of the room, and Ivanhoe and Felix walk up next to him. The three form a line, with arms crossed. They stand solemnly, and the camera zooms in and focuses in on them. As if they're in a funeral. What Freud calls the "death drive" is strong in white supremacy. The racist lives in a modern world where Enlightenment ideas of equality and dignity have triumphed. Their reactionary fantasies rest not only on the possibility of total annihilation of the current order, but these fantasies put themselves under constant threat, surveillance, and banishment from the public sphere. It is the ever-present possibility of death, which ups the ante of their commitment.

Minute 93

Ivanhoe, who is grimacing, moving his mouth without saying anything for at least 15 seconds, slowly walks away from Stallworth, shaking his head. He's struggling to say something. His mouth opens, but no sound comes out. He tries again. Nothing. "God," he finally says, walking away. We wait with anticipation. "America's going to hell in a handbasket," he declares. Ivanhoe's facial distortion, accompanied by his inability to say something of substance—apart from banalities like America is "going to hell"—is not only meant to invoke laughter in the audience, but it speaks to a larger fact about the banality of white supremacy. The performance is dramatic, but the philosophy is not especially complicated or sophisticated. Perhaps, you wonder, maybe the emptiness is the point? The emptiness of the ideas, the bankruptcy of ideology, is what makes racism accessible and simultaneously unresponsive to any logical critique or analysis. With this ideological structure, who could successfully convince the racist to change their ways?

Minute 94

The scene abruptly moves to another gathering—a radically different one—this one of members of the Colorado Springs Black Student Union. They're gathering in an apartment, listening to an older man, Jerome Turner (played by the Black Civil Rights icon and legendary actor Harry Belafonte). Turner is sitting in a suit and tie upon a wicker chair, speaking about an event that occurred fifty years before. He recalls how a seventeen-year-old Black friend of his, who was disabled, was falsely accused of and tried in court for raping a white woman. The all-white jury "deliberated for four minutes," he says, to audible gasps from the audience. Racism exposes the limits of the juridical system. It collapses the time we normally associate with the inner workings of justice—the slow and plodding movement of liberalism. At the same time, racist legal outcomes invigorate the populist who wants the law to work quickly, who is annoyed at its slow, technical, and messy nature. Legal processes involving elites—relating to political corruption, tax evasion, corporate malfeasance—take a long and arduous process. Appeals. Petitions. Reviews. In a racist system, however, 4 minutes is all it takes to convict someone of an imagined crime. The speed and violence of such legal processes are unquestionably unjust—but, on a deeper level, it provides a collective outlet for racist societies to insist on the myth that their legal structure is effective and efficient.

Minute 95

We have watched 94 minutes of *BlacKkKlansman*, but this is the first moment in the film where we see Klansmen dressed in their white robes. There we see Duke, who stands before a group of white men and tells them to take their masks off and put their hoods on. Behind Duke, we see a political poster on the wall: "re-elect Nixon and Agnew." The juxtaposition between the white hoods and the poster encapsulates a primary thesis of the film. There is a thin line between institutionalized white supremacy, conducted through the halls of political institutions and laws—slavery, segregation, mass incarceration—and its more populist, interpersonal offshoots. Incumbent Republican president Richard Nixon and his vice-president Spiro Agnew, first elected in 1968, ran for reelection in 1972 on a "law and order" platform. Law and order was a racially coded language for increasing the policing of Black communities that were engaged in urban uprisings and rebellions (in Detroit, Newark, Watts, Atlanta). Nixon was not Duke, who reveled in racist conspiracy. But Nixon nonetheless promised to use the power of the state to discipline and punish Black citizens. What is more terrifying and dangerous for democracy, minute 95 asks: the white hoods and robes of the Klan, which, through their wardrobe and words, give clear legibility to their racist beliefs and desires, or a politician who speaks in veiled language and works from within institutions? The one who works from within the party, or the one outside it?

Minute 96

The camera cuts between Turner continuing to lecture the Black students about his friend, who is "dragged out" of his home onto the street by a mob who "cut off his testicles," and Duke, who stands before a group of Klansmen, their hoods concealing their faces. Duke repeats something of both a prayer and exhortation, "God, give us true white men." Language and vivid detail like Turner's, no matter how brutal or horrific, have always been key tool in antiracist strategies of dismantling white supremacy. The racist, like

Duke, attempts to conceal their violence through ideologies of manhood and patriotism. But the antiracist explicitly names these ideologies to be responsible for that violence. At the same time, as Turner tells his story, we recognize that the precision and specificity with which the racist seeks to denigrate the Black body is connected to anxieties about their own identity. The rite of initiation for the Klan to be a "true white man," just as the symbolic act of lynching, would not be necessary—so suggests minute 96—if the racist believed the truth of that identity was unassailable. Uncertainty is what powers the racist machine, what fuels its assault on the Black body.

Minute 97

Now the camera cuts back to Turner, "They cut off his fingers," he continues, this time looking at us, the viewers. "And threw coal oil over his body. They lit a bonfire and raised him and lowered him over these flames over and over and over again." Minute by minute, the film implicates the viewer in considering uncomfortable truths, which they would rather avoid. For instance, there is a long-standing tendency for many self-proclaimed liberals to profess their outrage over racism, while simultaneously basking in heroic historical narratives of American democratic exceptionalism. "I know there are racists, but our country is committed to freedom and equality." But are these citizens truly aware of the machinations and dynamics of the racist machine? If they were, would they be as surprised—or better prepared—when they learn of the killing in broad daylight of a Black teen, Michael Brown, in Ferguson in 2015 by a white police officer, the rise of Trump in 2016, the march on Charlottesville in 2017, the murder of George Floyd and Breonna Taylor in 2020? Would a reimagined historical understanding lead to a better understanding of the present?

Minute 98

Turner holds up a large placard, which has a reprint of a lynching photo. He is surrounded by several Black Student Union members, doing the same thing. All of them look directly at the camera. Together, they become a postcard of witnessing, of remembering trauma. Trauma, in the words of literary theorist Cathy Caruth, is

> much more than a pathology, or the simple illness of a wounded psyche: it is always the story of a wound that cries out, that addresses us in the attempt to tell us of a reality or truth that is not otherwise available. This truth, in its delayed appearance and its belated address, cannot be linked only to what is known, but also to what remains unknown in our very actions and our language.[30]

Witnessing is, for this reason, a crucial theme in Black political thought. The witness braids together memory and experience to bring forth stories and narratives that are marginalized in popular memory. The act of witnessing at once lays claim to the dignity of those who experienced trauma—so that their lives are not effaced by hegemonic narratives that seek to render them nameless and inert—but also becomes a way to ensure that trauma does not immobilize citizens in the present. Witnessing gives meaning to the ineffable and renders meaningful what once appeared meaningless, or weighted down by nothing but pain.

Minute 99

Now we witness Duke's ceremony of initiating and baptizing Klan members, as each of them takes up their hood and receives a ladle of water from Duke's golden chalice. As each hood comes up, we are disoriented to find not a teeth-baring, disordered subject, but a seemingly calm and respectable middle-aged white man. In the background of this ceremony, we hear Turner recalling how, as he witnessed his friend's gruesome lynching, many white citizens stood by and did nothing. Nothing at all. Silence and secrecy are two boons for white supremacy; the full-fledged racist and the so-called moderate aren't as far apart as we may think. Just like the Klansman hides their identity under their hood, there is a long history of white moderates who in public bask in their innocence, in their desire to stay above the fray, as they witness racial inequality. No wonder, in the words of Martin Luther King, the Negro's great stumbling block in his stride toward freedom is not the White Citizen's Counciler or the Ku Klux Klanner, but the white moderate, who is more devoted to "order" than to justice; who prefers a negative peace which is the absence of tension to a positive peace which is the presence of justice; who constantly says: "I agree with you in the goal you seek, but I cannot agree with your methods of direct action"; who paternalistically believes he can set the timetable for another man's freedom; who lives by a mythical concept of time and who constantly advises the Negro to wait for a more convenient season."[31]

Shallow understanding from people of good will is more frustrating than absolute misunderstanding from people of ill will. Lukewarm acceptance is much more bewildering than outright rejection. As King rightly explains, silence is an implicit affirmation of the status quo. Secrecy helps maintain power by hiding its unseen inner workings from public view. Distinctions between private and public racism are less important than public action. Where does one stand when they witness racial violence? What are they hiding in public; making public in private?

Minute 100

The two narratives—Turner's memory and the Klan initiation ceremony—merge into one. At the center of this is D. W. Griffith's *Birth of a Nation*, which we see the newly inaugurated Klansmen watching. Turner tells his audience—and by extension, the viewer—what is historically accurate: the Klan, which fell into oblivion in the late nineteenth century, was, in fact, galvanized into rebirth by Griffith's *Birth of a Nation* in the 1910s. Turner says this at the very same moment we see newly baptized Klansmen (along with Walter, Connie, Felix, Ivanhoe, and Duke) eating, laughing, throwing popcorn around, and engaging in armchair criticism of its plot. "Today, they would call that kind of movie a blockbuster," Turner says, "Even the president of the United States, Woodrow Wilson, showed it at the White House." *BlacKkKlansman* is both a counternarrative to *Birth of a Nation*, as it is an account of how cultural images and myths—of which film is a part—are crucial components of American political identity. Spike Lee, for decades, has been developing a counternarrative of American racial politics, which often fell on deaf ears during the Reagan, Clinton, and Bush years. *BlacKkKlansman* is both a summary of the themes Lee has developed throughout his career—white racial innocence, racist aggression, Black power, US empire, toxic manhood—as well as it is a visual representation of how the United States had managed to elect its first Black president and a white nationalist in a span of eight years. Just as *Birth of a Nation*, managed to galvanize a movement, *BlacKkKlansman*—in the aftermath of Charlottesville and Trump—aims to do the same, but with a radically different purpose. To forge an antiracist consciousness.

Minute 101

We continue to see the Klansmen watching *Birth of a Nation*. The moment that really energizes them, where they all stand up together, clapping excitedly, is the scene when the Klansmen arrive on horseback to put one of the Black citizens "on trial." "String him up!" yell Connie, Felix, and Walter in unison, while the screen flashes, "Guilty." Notice the joy on their faces. This is not a grim and misguided exercise of duty, a tragic attachment to antiquated cultural traditions—as some conservatives would describe slavery and white racial violence. This is a festival. A moment of revelry and unadulterated joy.

Minute 102

"White Power! White Power!" they all chant in unison, as *Birth of a Nation* concludes. Stallworth, in terror, is secretly observing it all from a small window. The scene quickly cuts to Turner and his gathering: "that's why we're here today," he tells the students. "Black Power! Black Power! Black Power!" Attempts to create false equivalences between white and Black power are dubious, as minute 102 so powerfully explains. White power is driven by a desire to expunge Black life, while Black power counters this through a politics of self-defense. White power is aggressive and antidemocratic, while Black power earns its strength through pragmatism and solidarity among citizens. White power treats identity in essentialist terms, while Black power treats it as a political project. To say Black power, therefore, is not to engage in "reverse racism." Advocates of Black power don't call for Black racial supremacy; their aim is Black liberation in the face of white supremacy.

Minute 103

The Klansmen are now toasting champagne at the reception hall of the hotel. They're no longer in robes; now they're in pressed suits. Duke raises a glass and applauds them for being the "true white American race," for "never putting their country second." "America first!" they all chant, repeating Donald Trump's infamous campaign slogan of 2016. In a span of 20 minutes (beginning at minute 92), we see the easy and seamless conversion of white supremacy from a formless and chaotic mass to a structured, organized, and polished movement. Champagne replaces beer; suits replace biker jackets; a hotel room replaces an underground basement. On the one hand, little has changed. The ideology remains the same, the white supremacy as strong as ever. On the other hand, in the realm of appearances, nothing is the same.

Minute 104

Felix and Connie walk up to Duke, visibly starstruck by the Grand Wizard's appearance in Colorado. They invite him over for dinner, but Duke politely declines, referencing his packed schedule. Harnessing populist anger and resentment might be, at first, easy for the demagogue, but it is difficult to contain over the long run. The bitter taste of disappointment on Connie's face is palpable to the viewer. The elite status that the white supremacist (in this minute, Duke) represents is a status that is, ultimately, inaccessible to his followers, who can begin to feel betrayed insofar as their charismatic power over them wanes. Betrayal then becomes rage, which becomes uncontrollable. Before long, the elite is deposed by the same energy that put him into power in the first place. Here is a historical truth worth remembering. Fascist demagogues never have long periods of stable rule; the system that puts them in place is far too volatile, the relationship between ruler and ruled subject to irrevocable rupture. This means that the fascist leader is prone to irrational behavior and risk-taking; but it also means that there are always moments for antifascists to resist him.

Minute 105

The unnamed man who shows Connie how to use the C-4 explosive (see minute 88) slowly walks up to Felix and points out Zimmerman in the crowd. "He's a cop," the man says, referencing how Zimmerman had once arrested him for armed robbery. Within several seconds, Felix pieces everything together. He turns from Stallworth, guarding Duke, to Zimmerman, and recognizes that Ron Stallworth (whose apartment he had visited in minute 65) is the name of the Black police officer serving as Duke's police escort, and that Zimmerman and Stallworth are likely working together undercover. After 105 minutes the secret is finally out, a central narrative point of the film is resolved. But there is still something unsettling about Felix's lack of surprise. He looks stoically toward Zimmerman and begins to smile. Neither shocked nor troubled, Zimmerman is singularly focused on commencing Connie's terrorist act. *BlacKkKlansman*'s narrative is built around an undercover investigation, but, at minute 105, asks a difficult question: what if white racism is, fundamentally, undeterred by the law? What if the white racist doesn't care whether he is discovered or not? Investigated or tried? How does society contend with such attitudes?

Minute 106

Stallworth, recognizing something is amiss, walks up to Duke and asks him to take a Polaroid picture, saying that none of his friends would believe him if he told them that he was guarding a Klansman, let alone the Grand Wizard of the KKK. Stallworth gestures to Zimmerman (his cover has not yet been blown to anyone but Felix) and asks him to take the picture. The politics of the image is one more put on display—as a counternarrative to the lynching photographs that we have already been exposed to earlier in the film. Stallworth, like Spike Lee, wants to control the narrative on his terms, and define white supremacy from an antiracist perspective. Lee successfully accomplishes this not through an abstract or neutral perspective—not the perspective, in other words, of colorblindness. By giving texture to white supremacy through the lens of color-consciousness—its impact on the perpetrators and victims—Lee defends the idea of grounded political theory.

Minute 107

As soon as Zimmerman snaps the photo, Stallworth hugs Duke and the man standing next to him. He quickly runs up to and grabs the photo from Zimmerman. "What the hell did you just do, boy?" Duke asks him, furious. "Sir, if you lay a finger on me, I'll arrest your ass for assaulting a police officer," Stallworth replies. Stallworth seizes the frame—overturning the Jim Crow politics of the lynching postcard. No longer a passive, voiceless subject, Stallworth smiles warmly and wraps his arms around Duke, mocking him, while at the same time strategically and creatively working from within the bounds of legality and authority to do so. Stallworth, without sanction or approval from white supremacy, captures the discourse of freedom of expression, of rights, to make it work for him. Leveraging his right of creative, nonviolent self-expression, Stallworth at once positions himself as an ideal democratic citizen—he reminds Duke that violent intimidation is unacceptable—but uses this status in a way to call attention to Duke's antidemocratic attitudes.

Minute 108

From the other side of the banquet hall, Stallworth observes the unnamed man, charged with handling explosives and who exposed Zimmerman's identity to Felix, walking up to Connie's table, where he gives her the detonation control and tells her to begin her job. She walks out of the hotel. Stallworth nervously watches. The paternalism and orchestration of life are striking here. Authoritarian power (here, in the form of white supremacy) objectifies everything in sight. Connie, in Felix's eyes, is not his wife or companion; she is a pupil whose job is to carry out his will and direct orders, without complaint. Connie, for her part, is compliant. But as Lee makes clear throughout the film, her compliance stems not only from deep ideological commitment but also from a profound fear. The authoritarian creates the conditions for obedience because refusal is suicide.

Minute 109

As they eat lunch at a long banquet table, Felix turns to Zimmerman and asks him if he has met the man who claimed to be arrested by him. Zimmerman is confused, and Felix urges Zimmerman, whom he calls "Flip," not to be. Zimmerman's cover is blown, his identity exposed. And yet, the look on Zimmerman's face is one of confusion as well. Now that law enforcement has intervened officially, the investigation on display, what can be done? This is a question about the limits and capacities of state power. From Hobbes to Locke to Rousseau, a long-standing belief in modern political thought is that the political state is capable of upholding the social contract and maintaining order—through the threat of punishment and discipline. But what if these threats and mechanisms have no purchase on actors who don't recognize the state's authority, and subvert it at every turn?

Minute 110

Just at this moment, one of the Black waitstaff approaches the table and says there's a phone call for Felix. It's Connie. "Jesus, they have cops everywhere," she says inside a phone booth, panicking and in tears, as she watches a police car pass her, and as the Black student protest is picking up steam. "Somebody tipped them off." We feel Connie's anxiety, her withering commitment to the cause. This isn't surprising, given that authoritarianism creates total fear in its victims. Yet that total fear is a double-edged sword. It can create absolute obedience, just as it creates a spark of resistance. With the experience of total dread—with nothing to fear but fear itself—the victim of totalitarianism can engage in unexpected, even if risky, action, which might lead to revolutionary change. Connie, of course, is no revolutionary, but the affective structure that informs her panic is the same structure that leads some racists to become ex-racists, to abandon their cause. The fear that keeps them committed is the same thing that undoes their commitment.

Minute 111

Stallworth runs out of the hotel, jumps into his car, and speeds toward the Black student rally, where, once he arrives, he discovers that Patrice and her friend, Odetta, have already left, to take Turner back to his hotel. The anxiety Stallworth feels is palpable to the viewer, conjuring what critical race theorists understand as the idea of Black fugitivity. Political theorist Neil Roberts argues that such an idea informs some conceptions of Black freedom. Developing the idea of "freedom as marronage" (marronage is defined as a state of being inhabited by fugitive ex-slaves), Roberts writes, "Marronage is a multidimensional, constant act of flight . . . movement is the central principle . . . agents struggle psychologically, socially, metaphysically, and politically to exit slavery, maintain freedom, and assert a lived social space while existing in a liminal position."[32] Roberts describes these conditions through concrete examples of fleeing from racial enslavement, but we can extend his reasoning by understanding Black life in a racist society, in part, to be defined by a state of perpetual motion—escape from (potential) captivity or rushing toward solidarity in the face of catastrophe. The Black Lives Matter slogan "I Can't Breathe" thus takes on a different meaning in this context. The lack of breath is defined not simply by the suffocating experience of racism, but by the breathlessness of speed in resisting and organizing against domination.

Minute 112

Connie arrives at Patrice's house in her GMC pick-up truck. She's wearing a red dress, holding a leopard print bag, and is walking toward Patrice's house with a gait that appears as if she's arrived for her first day of work in a corporate office. The camera captures Connie's posture of self-possession to highlight a cruel irony at work. The racist patriarchy has incredible reach in all aspects of life. Connie feels self-worth only insofar as she contributes to the project of anti-Black violence. Indeed, her social status as a white woman, in the white supremacist imaginary, is dependent upon the extent to which she can inflict maximal Black pain, perhaps in an exemplary and disproportionate manner compared to her male counterparts. This grotesque dialectic is something she must master, become expert in, if she is to survive. White supremacy is like a corporation that includes marginalized subjects (like women) only insofar as their productivity level is exceptional.

Minute 113

Connie is about to stuff the C-4 into Patrice's mailbox as Patrice's red Volkswagen Beetle pulls up to her house. Panicking, Connie briskly walks off and hides behind the bushes. As Patrice and Odetta come out of the car, they discuss the importance of having a more intersectional approach to thinking about racial domination. "Next time, we should work on getting a sister in here. We need to be hearing their stories." Patrice and Odetta verbalize the Black feminist perspective that is a counterpoint to patriarchal politics. Their comments also call into question what viewers may be wondering throughout: whether Spike Lee himself has sufficiently developed a Black feminist practice of filmmaking in *BlacKkKlansman*. Clearly, Patrice is the figure of political consciousness and sophisticated critique; indeed, one can argue that her voice and story throughout the film offer an alternative to masculine images of freedom presented by the Klan and the CSPD. At the same time, the viewer wonders whether Patrice's vantage could have been more effectively highlighted, whether her intersectional struggles and resistance could have been better explored. This tension is unresolved, but minute 113 highlights it, as if to engage in an imminent, self-conscious critique of *BlacKkKlansman*'s own limitations and narrative inconsistencies.

Minute 114

Stallworth speeds to Patrice's house and sees Connie walking up. "You're under arrest," he screams, before he puts her arms around her back, wrestling her to the floor. "Help! You're hurting me!" she screams. "Where's the bomb? Where'd you put it?" Stallworth asks. At that very moment, two white police officers arrive at the scene and tell Stallworth to get up and put his hands over his head. "I'm undercover! I'm a cop,"

Stallworth yells, but they aim their guns straight at him. "He tried to rape me! Arrest him!" Connie screams. We have seen this racist trope—of Black male hypersexuality and violence—before. Both in the *BlacKkKlansman* and in US history. It is, as we've already seen, most famously articulated in *Birth of a Nation*, but it comes back with a vengeance time and time again. Against progressive accounts of historical development, eternal recurrence, Friedrich Nietzsche argues throughout his writings, is the process through which history becomes prologue; the past melds into the future. What does it mean to know that this is the case? Does one adopt a position of radical pessimism, insisting that all is lost and nothing could change? Does one instead become primarily attached to prophetic critique, drawing attention to the deleterious effects of this process, shedding light on its contours from different vantage points? Or does one act with the realization that the weight of history cannot be shed, but a utopian horizon, or radically different worlds, of being otherwise, must be imagined nonetheless?

Minute 115

Felix slowly pulls up to Patrice's house, with the C-4 detonator in hand. As he's doing this, the two white officers are viciously beating Stallworth, who is writhing in pain on the ground. Felix presses the trigger and Patrice's car explodes. Ron is on the floor, screaming "Patrice!" while Patrice gets off the ground and is confused. After preparing us for a seismic act of racist violence for 114 minutes, we witness firsthand the racist fantasy become reality. The explosion takes up the entire frame, the ball of fire saturates our eyes. But what's even more striking about the explosion is how little it changes. This is, at the heart, the radical nihilism of the racist position. Senseless violence, done with the sole purpose of inflicting terror and pain, will not create the white utopia racists imagine. Deep down, the racist knows this. In fact, racial violence will likely do the very opposite of galvanizing support—it will further ostracize racists from the mainstream, creating formidable coalitions between people who otherwise might be ideologically opposed. The racist thus precipitates the conditions for their own construction. Ironically, it must be this way because it is the provocative promise of, and ultimate realization of, violence that gives the racist attention in society. Without violence, they are nothing. But once they finally enact it, they are threatened out of existence.

Minute 116

Zimmerman arrives at the scene and yells at the two cops: "Hey! Hey! Stand down! Stand down!" "The Black guy's a cop?" one of the officers asks. Zimmerman unlocks Stallworth's handcuffs and glares at the officer, who genuinely appears stunned. The viewer has been prepared for this dynamic—a Black man being accosted by police, preemptively imagined as criminal—and yet there's something nonetheless tragic about witnessing it once more in minute 116. Even if the Black activist wants to uphold the norm, assume a position of exemplary patriotism, the success of this venture is always questionable. Consider, for example, that a figure like Martin Luther King Jr. can enact nonviolent civil disobedience in the name of US unity but still be deemed by J. Edgar Hoover as one of the most dangerous men alive. Or NFL quarterback Colin Kaepernick can take a knee during the national anthem over a football game—in the name of helping America live up to its democratic ideals—and still be deemed enemy number one, a traitor to the nation. Minute 116, in the final analysis, calls into question the ideal of Black assimilation and gradual reformism. Stallworth, a citizen of influence aiming to reform a racist system from the inside, is subject to the same fate as ordinary Black citizens—who have little social power.

Minute 117

Patrice and Stallworth are sitting at a bar, laughing, as the racist cop from the CSPD, Andy Landers, approaches them. Landers is drunk. "How often do you do that? Pull us over for nothing. Harass us?" Patrice asks him. Far from being apologetic or deferential, Landers is enraged at her question. "What I did to your girl the other night," he says to Stallworth—not even responding to Patrice—referencing the night he pulled Patrice over after Ture's speech, "I could do to any of you anytime, anyplace. That's my prerogative." Landers continues with teeth bared, "I could even bust a cap in your Black ass," he tells Stallworth. Having temporarily foiled the plans of white terrorists, Stallworth—and the viewer—is confronted with a far deeper and entrenched problem: racism within the state. White supremacists exist everywhere in society, but they are especially interested in infiltrating institutions of coercion—law enforcement, military, or national security. This is because these institutions harbor exorbitant power in the regulation of society and because they operate in clandestine ways, often avoiding political oversight and working within a code of secrecy. What makes these institutions effective at carrying out the work of the state is also what makes them attractive to reactionary forces. And yet, weeding out these forces from within these institutions is a tall order. For the ideal of accountability and bipartisanship—which would be undermined by exposing decay and corruption within their ranks—is what gives these institutions public legitimacy. This legitimacy would be threatened by more rigorous oversight. Secrecy reigns supreme.

Minute 118

Stallworth reveals that he is wearing a recording device, and now has Landers's confession on tape. "Did you get that?" He asks out loud, seemingly to no one in particular. But then we see it: members of the CSPD come out of the other booths in the bar. Out walks Chief Bridges, who places Landers under arrest for sexual harassment, battery, and intimidating a police officer. Everyone comes into Zimmerman's and Patrice's booth, toasting: "we did it!" This spirit of jubilation makes the viewer temporarily feel that all is whole, that justice has been executed, and that the rule of law is intact. Yet, given everything that we've seen throughout the film, the viewer is left feeling cold. Landers may be a bad apple, whose deeds are justly punished, but there's so much more at work, and so much more to be done. The institution remains. The structural inequality is still there. The two anonymous CSPD cops who seek to arrest Stallworth (minute 116), for instance, represent the larger problematic of structural racism that exists beyond Landers. And they are still at large. So, too, for that matter, is Duke.

Minute 119

Ron walks into the CSPD precinct the next morning, on top of the world. He receives a standing ovation from his coworkers. The temporary joy he feels is crushed at the very moment Bridges ushers Zimmerman and Stallworth into his office and regrets to inform them that, due to budget cuts and inflation, the Klan case is closed. "Besides, there no longer appears to be any credible threats," Bridges says. Bridges reminds us of what we already know: the prerogative of the state is to reproduce itself, to secure order. The larger, small "d" democratic question of justice is thus secondary to the need to secure legitimacy and crush external threats, who pose existential challenges to its well-being. If these threats aren't existential, however, they aren't treated with urgency. Budgets and personnel—the mechanisms of bureaucracy—begin to take hold and guide the decision-making process.

Minute 120

"And now," Bridges says, "I need you, Ron Stallworth, to destroy all evidence of this investigation." "We prefer that the public never knew about this investigation." Stallworth is dejected and in disbelief. Zimmerman, agitated, walks away in disgust. *BlacKkKlansman*, like all forms of cultural production, is partly a work of counter-memory-making, whose power comes from existing in a state of permanence, well past its immediate context of production. To appreciate this artifact, one must be able to preserve and disseminate it. But what happens if, like the evidence Bridges mentions, it is suppressed? Expunged? Or, even less dramatically, forgotten? Minute 120 reminds us of the fragility of culture in political action. To act you must be rooted. To be rooted you must remember. This is why cultural memory is a battlefield for and of politics.

Minute 121

Having been told to cease all communication with the Klan by his superiors, Stallworth sits at his desk pensively, looking repeatedly at his phone, which is ringing. Over and over again. The sounds punctuate the image of Stallworth getting up from his desk and shredding evidence, before he walks out of the building. And yet, the phone is still ringing, goading Stallworth into picking it up. We tend to center our understanding of politics from the perspective of actors, histories, and institutions—but what of objects? What happens if, following the French sociologist Bruno Latour, we view this from the perspective of the object? How does the existence of a phone—the very medium for communication—and its placement in an office, its centrality in the organization of community, intervene to make a demand upon us? Technology, in other words, begins not only to extend and augment the possibilities for action but activates us, bringing forward choices and possibilities we'd like to avoid.[33] The phone speaks, and Stallworth listens. He picks it up.

Minute 122

"Mr. Duke," says Stallworth on the phone, while trying desperately to contain his laughter, with Zimmerman and other officers surrounding him, "I'm sorry we didn't get to spend more one-on-one time together." The audience is in on the joke because Stallworth did spend extended time with Duke during the convention in Colorado Springs—even if only Duke doesn't yet know it. The competing and unequal perspectives—Stallworth needs to monitor Duke at all times, but Duke doesn't need to know who or where Stallworth is—is a theme of Black culture, what sociologist W. E. B. Du Bois calls in *The Souls of Black Folk*, the power of "second sight."[34] To survive in a racist society, Black citizens must work to know that society, and its majority, intimately and deeply—its manners of speech, dress, movements, tastes, and preferences. On the other hand, white citizens, who form the majority, can remain oblivious to its inner workings, especially as it pertains to race.

Minute 123

Stallworth baits Duke one last time: "Did you ever get the name of that [Black] detective," he asks? The detective is "Ron Stallworth," he says, "you racist . . . redneck, inchworm . . . motherfucker!" he yells, as he slams down the receiver. The camera cuts to Duke, who looks into the distance as he sits in his empty office. Duke's bewilderment can mean one of two things. On the one hand, perhaps he feels genuine disbelief. Duke has recognized that he has been duped by Stallworth—thus, undermining racist narratives of white superiority, of innate racist intelligence, upon which his movement is based. On the other hand, perhaps it's not disbelief but silence and apathy that Duke feels. Knowing that his status and power have nothing to do with some intrinsic truth about Black inferiority and white superiority—but instead, his ability to convince his followers that such a distinction exists—Duke remains perfectly content being misled by Stallworth, as long as Duke's followers don't know. This possibility is priced in by racist elites. Either way—whether Duke is confused, angry, or apathetic—his status among his followers is unchanged. He remains in his office. He is not jailed. His racist project continues unimpeded.

Minute 124

Patrice and Stallworth are sitting in the kitchen, when Patrice asks him if he has resigned both from the Klan and from the CSPD, as if the two, despite their differences, share problematic histories regarding anti-Black violence. Their conversation is interrupted by a loud knock on the door. Alarmed, Patrice and Stallworth take out their guns, open the door, and, in a dream-like sequence, they are frozen, pointing their weapons as if they are trying to subdue an enemy. They move, still frozen, toward a window, outside of which they—along with the viewers—

see a Klan cross-burning ceremony. "Blood and Soil," the Klansmen chant. The film vacillates in tone between thriller and comedy, but minute 124 embraces elements of surrealism to stress the collapsing space between past and future. This is to emphasize that Stallworth and Patrice—like many Black citizens—exist in a state where they must be on guard about American fictions—of progress, of reconciliation, redemption, or peace.

Minute 125

The fictional blood and soil chant in the film cuts to real footage of a blood and soil chant, which took place a year before *BlacKkKlansman* was released: in Charlottesville, Virginia, on August 12, 2017, when white supremacists rallied as part of what was called "Unite the Right." "White lives matter!" "Jews will not replace us," the white crowd shouts. The fictional representation of *BlacKkKlansman* ends, and reality abruptly kicks in. The surreal nightmare that Black citizens experience (as indicated by minute 124) now becomes the historical nightmare of all Americans. How striking is it to see—almost fifty years after the film is set—that white supremacy, despite being imagined as beyond the pale and in the dustbin of history, is alive and well in 2017. The film now takes on a new urgency, making its intentions clear about its purpose. Watch *BlacKkKlansman*, it says, to better understand how we got from Nixon to Trump, from Duke to Charlottesville.

Minute 126

Images of violence saturate the screen. Antiracist counter-protestors chanting "Black Lives Matter," are beaten and assaulted by far-right terrorists. The footage is raw, and unfiltered. Overwhelming. We are engulfed in the flames, fists,

94   BLACKKKLANSMAN

crowds, batons. It's hard to watch, but we still can't look away. We know this happened—this is archival footage, which was front-page news at the time. This framing of reality—we rewatch it with 125 minutes of *BlacKkKlansman* behind us—implicates us into taking a stand about our political convictions. If we thought the fictional narrative of *BlacKkKlansman* was funny or a matter of history, how do we respond now? If, however, we weren't amused, then do we feel vindicated? Apathetic? Hopeless? Or emboldened to act?

Minute 127

The frame moves away from the violence on the street, to the bastions of political power. "You had a group on one side that was bad," says the then president Trump, at a news conference at New York's Trump Tower the same day, surrounded by Secretary of the Treasury Stephen Mnuchin (who is Jewish) and Secretary of Transportation Elaine Chao (who is of Asian descent) "and you had a group on the other side that was also very violent." "Not all of these people were white supremacists. You also had people that were very fine people." Trump continues. As he speaks, images of men in Charlottesville walking with swastikas saturate the screen, undercutting his false equivalences between racism and antiracism. The image then cuts to the real David Duke, whom we know from the movie, and who was present at Charlottesville on August 12, 2017. Duke, standing in a T-shirt, in front of reporters and supporters says that he believes "this is a first step toward making a realization of something that Trump alluded to earlier on the campaign trail, which is . . . taking America back." The lines between Trump and Duke are collapsed. Racism is closer to power than ever before, no longer lurking in the darkness, in basements, behind closed doors. It's out in the open. Proud. Emboldened.

Minute 128

A car rams into a crowd of counter-protesters at Charlottesville, killing a white woman, Heather Heyer. We see a photo of Heyer on the screen (1985–2017), "rest in power." Heyer's photo turns into a photo of the American flag, which, slowly, over the course of 10 seconds, is progressively darkened. The stars and stripes of the flag turn to black and white. The title of the film, *BlacKkKlansman*, saturates the screen in block letters. The movie ends, in darkness and blood, but also in memory of antiracism. This is the memory that the film tries to refine and reproduce in visual terms, as it works against the legacy of amnesia, of forgetting racial terror. Sometimes binaries must be established. They are important to frame the costs of action or inaction. What kind of nation at once produces Duke, Trump, and Charlottesville, and its opposite—Patrice Dumas, Ron Stallworth, Flip Zimmerman? What future is possible or impossible? The image fades to black. You are left to decide the answer.

NOTES

1 Jean-Paul Sartre, *Anti-Semite and Jew* (New York: Schocken Books, 1948), 12.

2 James Baldwin, "Many Thousands Gone," in *The Price of the Ticket: Collected Nonfiction: 1948–1985* (New York: Beacon Press, 1985), 75.

3 Baldwin, "Many Thousands Gone," 77–8.

4 Frederick Douglass, "The Meaning of July Fourth for the Negro" (1852) in *Frederick Douglass, Selected Speeches and Writings* (Chicago: Chicago Review Press, 1999), 188–206.

5 James C. Scott, *Domination and the Arts of Resistance: Hidden Transcripts* (New Haven: Yale University Press, 1992), 4.

6 Robin D. G. Kelley, *Race Rebels: Culture, Politics and the Black Working Class* (New York: Free Press, 1996), 31.

7 See "Alienated Labor," in *Karl Marx: Selected Writings*, ed. David McLellan (New York: Oxford University Press, 2000), 83–122.

8 Ralph Ellison, *Going to the Territory* (New York: Vintage, 1986), 109.

9 Ella Baker, "Developing Community Leadership," 1970, https://www.crmvet.org/info/70_baker_community_ldsp.pdf.

10 Michael Dawson, *Black Visions: The Roots of Contemporary African-American Ideologies* (Chicago: University of Chicago Press, 2003), 2.

11 Malcolm X, "The Ballot or the Bullet," in *Malcolm X Speaks: Selected Speeches and Statements* (New York: Grove Press, 1965), 33.

12 Lewis R. Gordon, *Fear of Black Consciousness* (New York: Farrar, Straus and Giroux, 2022), 19.

13 Ralph Ellison, *The Collected Essays of Ralph Ellison*, ed. John C. Callahan (New York: Modern Library, 1995), 161.

14 Frantz Fanon, *Wretched of the Earth* (New York: Grove Press, 2004), 15.

15 Niccolo Machiavelli, *The Prince* (Cambridge: Cambridge University Press, 1988), 63.

16 James Baldwin, *The Fire Next Time* (New York: Vintage, 1992), 103.

17 Karen Brodkin, *How Jews Became White Folks & What That Says about Race in America* (New Brunswick: Rutgers University Press, 1998), 282.

18 Charles Mills, *The Racial Contract* (Ithaca: Cornell University Press, 1997), 3–5.

19 Ben Tillman, "Lynch Law," *The Congressional Record—Senate*, 59th Cong., 2nd Sess., vol. 41, pt. 2 (January 1907), 1441.

20 Ida B. Wells, *Southern Horrors: Lynch Law in All Its Phases* (1892), http://www.digitalhistory.uh.edu/disp_textbook.cfm ?smtid=3&psid=3614.

21 Sartre, *Anti-Semite and Jew*, 6.

22 Ellison, *Going to the Territory*, 145.

23 Hannah Arendt, *On Violence* (New York: Harcourt, 1970), 44.

24 W. E. B. Du Bois, *The Souls of Black Folk* (1903) (New York: Dover, 1994).

25 Nancy Fraser, "Social Justice in the Age of Identity Politics: Redistribution, Recognition, and Participation," in *Redistribution or Recognition: A Political-Philosophical Exchange*, ed. Nancy Fraser and Axel Honneth (New York: Verso, 2003), 92

26 James Baldwin, "The American Dream and the American Negro," in *The Price of the Ticket*, 410.

27 Hannah Arendt, *The Origins of Totalitarianism* (New York: Harcourt, Brace and Jovanovich, 1973), 464.

28 Ralph Ellison, "Invisible Man," in *The Collected Essays*, 373.

NOTES

29 Martin Luther King Jr., "Letter from a Birmingham Jail," (1963), in *A Testament of Hope*, ed. James M. Washington (San Francisco: Harper Collins, 1986), 295.

30 Cathy Caruth, *Unclaimed Experience: Trauma, Narrative, and History* (Baltimore: Johns Hopkins University Press, 2016), 4.

31 King, "Letter from a Birmingham Jail."

32 Neil Roberts, *Freedom as Marronage* (Chicago: University of Chicago Press, 2015), 10.

33 Bruno Latour, *Reassembling the Social: An Introduction to Actor-Network Theory* (Oxford: Oxford University Press, 2007),

34 Du Bois, *The Souls of Black Folk*, 2.

INDEX

accountability 88
act of witnessing 75
Afropessimism 26
American culture 62
anti-Black
    attitudes 54
    dehumanization 5
    societies 25
    violence 34, 45, 63, 66,
      84, 92
anti-Blackness 22, 25
antilynching 22
antiracist/antiracism 28, 94–5
    Black-Jewish antiracist
      alliance 49
    commitments 68
    consciousness 77
    counter-protestors 93
    movements 22
    projects 5
    strategies 73
    struggles 39
Anti-Semite and Jew (Sartre) 3
anti-Semitic/Semitism 47–8,
    55
    imagination 47
    racism 28
antislavery 22
apocryphal story 59
Arendt, Hannah 51, 58, 61,
    65, 67

artistic choices 43–4
Austin, J. L. 18
authoritarian power 82

baboons 30
Baker, Ella 16–17
Baldwin, James 2, 7, 9, 33, 60
The Ballot or the Bullet
    (Malcolm X) 23
bebop musicians 15
betrayal 67, 79
bipartisanship 88
The Birth of a Nation (Griffith)
    3, 4, 8, 77–8, 86
Black
    assimilation 6, 87
    autonomy 20
    culture 15, 30, 62
    empowerment 25
    feminist practice 85
    freedom 6–7, 70, 83
    ideological diversity 18
    liberation 14, 16, 41, 53,
      78
    male hypersexuality and
      violence 86
    political thought 20, 53,
      70, 75
    power 18, 21–3, 33, 54,
      77–8
    racial supremacy 78

INDEX

radicalism 13–14, 22, 53
self-defense and self-
   determination 13
student protest 83
Student Union 16, 66, 72,
   75
Black-Jewish
   antiracist alliance 49
   solidarity 28, 34
Black Lives Matter 13, 84, 93
Blackness 17, 19, 25, 32–3,
   42, 52, 54, 59
Black Skin, White Masks
   (1952) 19
Boston Tea Party 65
Brodkin, Karen 34
Brown v. Board of Education
   (1954) 2

capitalism 5, 12–13, 21
Caruth, Cathy 75
Chao, Elaine 94
Citizen Councils 70
civil rights 22–3
   legislation 55
   movement 11–12, 20, 24
   protestors 55
Civil Rights Act of 1964 4
code of secrecy 51, 88
Colorado Springs Black Student
   Union 72
Colorado Springs Police 4, 67
Colorado Springs Police
   Department (CSPD) 6,
   10, 27–8, 34, 40, 43, 66,
   68–9, 85, 88–9, 92
Cornelius Brothers & Sister
   Rose 26
corporate malfeasance 72
corruption 72, 88

counter-memory-making 90
culture wars 63

Davis, Angela 16
Dawson, Michael 17
decolonization 20
dehumanization 5, 10, 21
detachment 35
*Domination and the Arts of
   Resistance* (Scott) 11
double-consciousness 54
Douglass, Frederick 10, 21,
   53
Du Bois, W. E. B. 54, 91

Ellison, Ralph 15, 26, 49, 62
Enlightenment 30, 38, 71
enslavement 20, 62, 84
equality 52, 54, 69, 71, 74
   Black 7
   economic 14
   law enforcement 7

Fair Housing Act of 1968 4
Fanon, Frantz 19–20, 31
fascist demagogues 78
Fear of Black Consciousness
   (2022) 25
feminism 18
The Fire Next Time (1963)
   33
Floyd, George, murder of 74
Fraser, Nancy 57
freedom as marronage, idea
   of 83

Garvey, Marcus 54
gay liberation 52
Gone with the Wind (1936) 1
Griffith, D. W. 3, 8, 77

Harrison, Hubert 54
hierarchy 50, 52, 60
Hobbes, Thomas 82
Holocaust 47
Hoover, J. Edgar 13, 87
Hudson, Hosea 54
hypersexuality 8, 86

incorporation 5
inequality
racial 4, 38, 47–8, 76
structural 89
intimidation 70, 81

jazz 14–15
Jews 4, 30, 34, 47, 50, 93
Jim Crow 11
mobs 55
politics of lynching postcard 81
segregation 2, 4, 36

Kelley, Robin D. G. 11–12
King, Martin Luther, 76
King, Martin Luther, Jr., 53, 64, 87
Klan cross-burning ceremony 93
Ku Klux Klan 28, 76

labor 21–2, 37, 53, 67
Landers, Andy 11, 24, 27, 50, 88–9
Latour, Bruno 91
law and order 14, 73
Lee, Spike 2, 22, 44, 77, 81–2, 84, 85
The Leopard's Spots (Dixon) 8
liberalism 4, 69–70, 72
liberation

Black 14, 16, 41–2, 53, 67, 78
gay 52
Linnaeus, Carl 46
Little Rock Central High School, Arkansas 2
Little Rock Nine 2
Locke, John 40, 82
Lost Cause (Mitchell) 1
lynching 2, 22, 45, 60, 74–6, 81
lynch mobs 45, 70

Machiavelli, Niccolo 32
Malcolm X 23, 54
manhood 35, 60, 74, 77
marginalized citizens 69
Marx, Karl 12, 54
mass incarceration 2, 73
mass migration 37
Mills, Charles 40–1
Mnuchin, Stephen 94
moderate white majority 38

nationhood 60
Nazi concentration camp 21, 58
neo-Nazis 36
Newton, Huey 21
Nietzsche, Friedrich 86
Night Riders 70
Nixon, Richard 13, 73, 93
Nkrumah, Kwame 16
nonviolent self-expression 81
NORAD (North American Aerospace Defense Command) 65

O'Hara, Scarlett 1–2
On Violence (Arendt) 51
organized violence 65

INDEX

Origins of Totalitarianism (Arendt) 58

Parsons, Lucy 54
paternalism 82
patriarchy 8, 45, 84
patriotism 21, 48, 74, 87
pluralism 36, 69
police brutality 2, 14, 24, 27–8, 67
police power 51
policing the police 24
political education in art 43–4
political filmmaking 2
political radicalism 15
Politics as a Vocation (Weber) 65
post-Reconstruction era 8
post-Second World War era 58
pragmatism 15, 53, 78
The Prince (Machiavelli) 32
professionalism 70
psychological domination 19
public legitimacy 88

race/racial/racism 2–4, 6–7, 9, 22, 32, 36, 38, 60, 71, 83, 94
assimilation 5
authoritarianism 11
capitalism 5
conscious programs 33
contract 40–1
Darwinism 45, 46
enslavement 62, 84
and gender 45
inequality 4, 38, 47, 76
integration 6
justice 4, 38
metaphysics of 62

private and public, distinctions 76
problem 4
progress 5, 20
reverse 78
social structures of 43
terror 95
traitors 40
violence 45, 60, 76, 78, 87
war 22, 44
Race Rebels: Culture, Politics, and the Black Working Class (Kelley) 12
The Racial Contract (Mills) 39
radical nihilism 86
rage 3, 20, 35, 67, 79
respectability 6, 43
reverse racism 78
revolutionary language 19
Roberts, Neil 83
Rousseau, Jean-Jacques 40, 82

Sartre, Jean-Paul 3, 48
secrecy 76, 88
segregation 2, 4, 34, 36, 73
self-examination 42
self-hood 49
self-possession 22, 84
self-proclaimed liberals 74
sensational deeds 57
sexual harassment 89
Shepherd, Cybill 8
slavery 1, 10, 47, 73, 78, 84
social identities 42–3
Socrates 64
solidarity 11, 21–2, 27–8, 34, 78, 84
The Souls of Black Folk (Du Bois) 54, 91

structural racism 89
super predators 4

tax evasion 72
Taylor, Breonna, murder of 74
thoughtlessness, problem of 67
threat
    of disruption 23
    of punishment and discipline 82
    of violence 23, 69
Three Strikes Laws 27
Tillman, Ben 45
totalitarianism 61, 83
transformative movement 42
trauma 24, 75
Trump, Donald 13, 44, 74, 77–8, 93–5
Ture, Kwame 15–23, 26, 38, 41

uncertainty 74
Universal Declaration of Human Rights 58
urban uprisings and rebellions 73
US slavery in 1852 10

vernacular style 63
Vietnam War 5, 21
violence 31, 45–6, 57, 86–7
    anti-Black racial 45, 63, 66, 76, 78, 84, 86, 92
    in the colonies 31
    Klan 40

motivated reactionaries 45
objects of 63
organized 65
racial 60, 76, 78, 87
right-wing 65
state-sanctioned 22
on the street 94
threat of 23, 69
visual symbols in revolutionary movements 21
Voting Rights Act of 1965 4

Weber, Max 65
Wells, Ida B. 45
White Anglo-Saxon Protestant (WASP) 49
white civilization 50
white hoods and poster, juxtaposition between 73
white nationalism 22, 44
whiteness 17, 32, 34, 56–7, 59
white supremacist/ supremacy 2–3, 14–15, 19, 21–2, 28–30, 34, 36, 39–40, 45–6, 49, 50, 53, 56, 59, 63, 65, 69, 71, 73, 76, 78–9, 81–2, 84, 88, 93–4
white terrorism 45
Wilderson, Frank 26
Wilson, Woodrow 77
womanhood 16, 45
Wretched of the Earth (1961) 31